TOP 100
DESSERTS

TOP
100
DESSERTS

SAFEWAY/GOOD HOUSEKEEPING

Published exclusively for
Safeway
6 Millington Road, Hayes, Middlesex UB3 4AY
by Ebury Press
A division of Random House
20 Vauxhall Bridge Road
London SW1V 2SA

First published 1993

Edited by Felicity Jackson and Beverly Le Blanc
Designed by Peartree Design Associates
Special photography by Ken Field
Food stylist Kerenza Harries
Photographic stylists Sue Russell and Suzy Gittins

The paper in this book is acid-free

Typeset by Textype Typesetters, Cambridge
Printed in Italy

ISBN 0 09 182105 3

COOKERY NOTES

All spoon measures are level unless otherwise stated.

Size 2 eggs should be used except when otherwise stated.

Granulated sugar is used unless otherwise stated.

The oven should be preheated to the required
temperature unless otherwise stated.

Contents

FOREWORD

TOP 100 DESSERTS is one of a popular new series of colourful and practical cookery books created for Safeway customers. It contains 100 *Good Housekeeping* dessert recipes, ranging from the refreshingly light and healthy to rich and sumptuous ones.

The Good Housekeeping Institute is unique in the field of food and cookery, and every recipe has been created and double-tested in the Institute's world-famous kitchens, using readily available ingredients.

As well as all the family favourites, there are exciting ideas for using the many exotic fruits available nowadays, plus mouthwatering cheesecakes and gâteaux for those special occasions when you want to impress your family and friends.

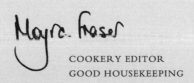

COOKERY EDITOR
GOOD HOUSEKEEPING

FRUDITÉS

SERVES 6

DIP:
150 ml (5 fl oz) double cream
150 ml (5 fl oz) soured cream
2 × 15 ml tbs icing sugar, sifted
FRUIT:
2 crisp eating apples, unpeeled but
    quartered and cored,
2 bananas, peeled and cut into 4 cm (1½ in) chunks
225 g (8 oz) apricots, quartered and stoned
175 g (6 oz) seedless black or green grapes
225 g (8 oz) strawberries, hulled
2 starfruit, peeled and sliced
3 ripe, figs, halved
50 g (2 oz) Cape gooseberries, (optional)
juice of 1 lemon

1. To make the dip, whip the two creams and icing sugar together in a bowl until standing in soft peaks. Pipe or spoon the mixture into six individual dishes.
2. Arrange the fruit on individual serving plates or one large plate and sprinkle immediately with lemon juice to prevent discoloration.
3. Place a dish of cream dip next to each plate of fruit and serve immediately. Use fingers or small fondue forks to dunk the fruit into the cream dip.

COOK'S TIP This is a deliciously refreshing dessert to serve after a rich main course. Try using fromage frais in the dip, instead of the double cream, for a lighter alternative.

9

Frudités

FRUIT IN FRAMBOISE

SERVES 8

900 g (2 lb) strawberries, washed
450 g (1 lb) raspberries, washed
6 × 15 ml tbs Framboise (raspberry liqueur)
6 × 15 ml tbs lemon juice
25 g (1 oz) icing sugar, sifted
single cream, to serve

1. Halve any large strawberries and mix together with 225 g (8 oz) raspberries.
2. Purée the remaining raspberries in a blender or food processor with the Framboise, lemon juice and icing sugar. Sieve over the fruit mixture. Stir lightly to mix without breaking up the fruit.
3. Cover and chill overnight. Serve with single cream.

VARIATION Instead of pouring the Framboise sauce over the strawberries and raspberries, serve it up as a dip accompanied with fresh fruits (see Frudités, page 9)

FRUIT IN SUMMER SAUCE

SERVES 8

225 g (8 oz) redcurrants, washed
450 g (1 lb) fresh raspberries, washed
115 g (4 oz) caster sugar
3 × 15 ml tbs water
4 × 15 ml tbs Kirsch
900 g (2 lb) mixed soft summer fruit, prepared
whipped cream, to serve

1. To make the sauce, strip the redcurrants from their stalks with a fork. Place in a saucepan with the raspberries and sugar.
2. Add the water and heat gently until the juices just begin to run, stirring occasionally. Pour into a food processor and blend until the mixture is smooth.
3. Push through a nylon sieve to remove the pips. Cool and stir in the Kirsch.
4. Divide the remaining fresh fruit among individual serving bowls and pour the sauce over the top. Chill, then serve with whipped cream.

COOK'S TIP As this Summer Sauce is made by blending fresh raspberries, it is an ideal way of using up over-ripe fruits.

POACHED PEARS WITH APRICOTS

SERVES 4

25 g (1 oz) butter or margarine
25 g (1 oz) preferably soft brown sugar
1 × 15 ml tbs lemon juice
150 ml (5 fl oz) water
675 g (1½ lb) ripe but firm pears, peeled, quartered and cored
50 g (2 oz) no-soak dried apricots, finely chopped
1 × 15 ml tbs Grand Marnier or brandy
chopped nuts, to decorate
ice cream or fresh cream, to serve

1. Put the butter, sugar and lemon juice in a pan with the water. Heat gently until the sugar dissolves, stirring.
2. Halve each pear quarter again if large. Add the pears and apricots to the syrup. Cover and simmer for 7-10 minutes, or until the pears are just tender. Stir in the Grand Marnier.
3. Serve hot, sprinkled with chopped nuts and topped with ice cream or fresh cream.

Fruit in Summer Sauce

Yogurt Rice Compote

SERVES 4

439 g can creamed rice
150 ml (5 fl oz) Greek-style yogurt
finely grated rind of 1 lemon
12 ratafia biscuits
2 × 15 ml tbs lemon juice
4 × 15 ml tbs jelly marmalade

1. Mix together the rice, yogurt and lemon rind. Divide between four 150 ml (5 fl oz) ramekins. Decorate with ratafias.
2. Heat the lemon juice with the marmalade in a small saucepan. Boil gently for a few minutes to reduce, then spoon over the ratafias.
3. Chill the compotes until ready to serve. If time is short, however, place in the freezer for a few minutes to chill.

Damask Cream

SERVES 4

600 ml (20 fl oz) single cream
3 × 15 ml tbs caster sugar
2 × 5 ml tsp rennet
large pinch of freshly grated nutmeg
1 × 15 ml tbs brandy
4 × 15 ml tbs double or clotted cream
rose petals, to decorate (optional)

1. Put the cream and 2 × 15 ml tbs of the sugar in a saucepan. Heat gently until tepid and the sugar dissolves, stirring. Stir in the rennet, nutmeg and brandy, then pour carefully into a serving dish.
2. Leave for 2-3 hours, until set. Do not disturb the junket during this time or it will not set properly.

Damask Cream

3. When the junket is set, mix the remaining sugar and double cream together. Spoon over the top of the junket and decorate with rose petals, if liked.

COOK'S TIP When the cream mixture is tepid it will register 36.9°C/98.4°F on a sugar thermometer, or not feel hot or cold if you put your finger in it.

Hot Pineapple and Banana Salad

SERVES 4

25 g (1 oz) butter or margarine
1 × 5 ml tsp soft light brown sugar
1 small pineapple, about 900 g (2 lb), peeled, cored and sliced
4 small bananas, about 450 g (1 lb) total weight, peeled and thickly sliced
2 × 15 ml tbs rum or orange juice
COCONUT SAUCE:
50 g (2 oz) creamed coconut, broken into pieces
75 ml (3 fl oz) boiling water
sugar to taste

1. Melt the butter in a large frying pan. Add the brown sugar and heat for 1 minute, stirring. Add the pineapple and cook gently for 3-4 minutes until it begins to soften and brown.
2. Stir in the banana chunks and sauté for 3 minutes, stirring gently so you do not break up the fruit. Pour in the rum or orange juice.
3. To make the coconut sauce, place the creamed coconut and the boiling water in a small saucepan. Stir until smooth. Add a pinch of sugar to taste. Gently bring to the boil, then simmer for 1 minute. Serve the sauce poured over the fruit.

COOK'S TIP Leftover creamed coconut will keep in the refrigerator for up to 3 months.

FRUIT SALAD WITH GINGER

SERVES 8

50 g (2 oz) caster sugar
150 ml (5 fl oz) water
grated rind and juice of 1 lemon
2 pieces stem ginger (from a jar of ginger in
     syrup), finely chopped
4 × 15 ml tbs ginger wine
675 g (1½ lb) lychees
3 ripe mangoes, peeled
432 g can pineapple slices
     in natural juice
4 ripe kiwi fruit, peeled

1. Put the sugar in a pan with 150 ml (5 fl oz)
water and the lemon rind and juice. Heat
gently until the sugar dissolves, stirring. Bring
to the boil, then simmer for 1 minute. Remove
from the heat and stir in the chopped ginger
and ginger wine. Leave to cool.
2. Peel the lychees, cut in half and remove the
shiny stones. Cut the mango flesh away from
the stones, then cut the flesh into cubes.
3. If using fresh pineapple, peel, slice and
remove the tough core from each slice. Cut the
pineapple slices into cubes. Thinly slice the
kiwi fruit and halve the slices.
4. Mix together the fruit and syrup. Cover and
chill for several hours to allow the flavours to
develop.

VARIATIONS Add 50 g (2 oz) Cape
gooseberries to decorate the salad. Peel back
each calyx to form a 'flower' and clean the
orange berry by wiping with a damp cloth.
     Use fresh pineapple, if preferred.

Fruit Salad with Ginger

15

Marinated Fruits

SERVES 6-8

900 g (2 lb) fresh raspberries or a mixture of
 summer fruits, such as strawberries,
 blackberries and blackcurrants
75 g (3 oz) caster sugar
about 300 ml (10 fl oz) red wine

1. Pick over the fruit. Cut the strawberries in half,
if using. Layer the fruit and sugar in a bowl. Pour
the wine over the fruit so the fruit is covered.
2. Cover tightly and store in the refrigerator for
up to 24 hours.

Compote

SPRING

SERVES 6

1 quantity Sugar Syrup (see opposite page)
40 g (1½ oz) fresh ginger root, peeled and
 finely shredded
1.4 kg (3 lb) rhubarb, cut into 5 cm (2 in) pieces

1. Make the syrup in a wide saucepan. Add the
ginger and cook gently for 2–3 minutes.
2. Add just enough rhubarb to make a single
layer. Cook gently for 5-6 minutes until just

Marinated Fruits

tender, turning the pieces frequently. Transfer to a serving dish. Continue cooking the rhubarb in batches.

3. Boil the syrup until reduced and slightly thickened, then pour over the rhubarb. Serve the compote hot or cold.

SUMMER

SERVES 6

I quantity Sugar Syrup (see right)
450 g (I lb) ripe peaches or nectarines, halved, stoned, skinned and cut into thick slices
450 g (I lb) ripe apricots, skinned, halved and stoned
450 g (I lb) dark cherries, stoned

1. Make the sugar syrup in a shallow, wide saucepan. Add the peach slices and cook gently for 10-15 minutes until barely tender. Add the apricots and cook for a further 5 minutes until the apricots just begin to soften.

2. Add the cherries and cook just long enough to soften them without losing their colour, about 3 minutes. Transfer the fruits and syrup to a serving bowl. Leave to cool, then chill.

AUTUMN

SERVES 6-8

I quantity Sugar Syrup (see right)
juice of I lemon
450 g (I lb) small ripe, but firm pears
450 g (I lb) dessert apples, such as Cox or Russet
450 g (I lb) Victoria plums, skinned and stoned

1. Make the sugar syrup in a shallow, wide saucepan, adding the lemon juice. Thinly peel the pears, cut into halves and remove the centre core (if only large pears are available, cut the pears into quarters). Add the pears to the syrup and cook very gently for about 10-15 minutes until barely tender.

2. Meanwhile, core the apples. Cut the apples into halves, then cut into slices across the halves. Add the apple slices to the pan and cook for about 5 minutes until the apple slices are just tender. Add the plums and cook for a further 5 minutes.

3. Carefully transfer the fruits and syrup to a serving bowl, taking care not to break up the fruit. Serve hot or cold.

WINTER

SERVES 6-8

I quantity Sugar Syrup (see below)
450 g (I lb) kumquats, thickly sliced
450 g (I lb) clementines, peeled and segmented
175 g (6 oz) seedless black grapes
175 g (6 oz) seedless green grapes
175 g (6 oz) cranberries

1. Make the sugar syrup in a shallow, wide saucepan. Add the kumquats, cover and cook gently for about 15-20 minutes until barely tender.

2. Add the clementines and grapes, then cook for a further 5 minutes, gently turning the fruits in the syrup and taking care not to break them up. Add the cranberries and cook the compote for about 5 minutes until softened. Carefully transfer the fruits and syrup to a serving bowl. Serve hot or cold.

SUGAR SYRUP

225 g (8 oz) granulated sugar
300 ml (10 fl oz) cold water

Put the sugar and cold water in a saucepan. Heat very gently until the sugar has completely dissolved. Bring to the boil and boil the syrup for 1 minute.

Stuffed Figs

SERVES 8

250 g packet ricotta cheese, at room
   temperature
150 ml (5 fl oz) double or whipping cream
few drops of almond flavouring
16 fresh figs
fig or vine leaves and rose petals, to serve

1. Beat the ricotta cheese in a bowl until soft.
Whip the cream in another bowl until just
standing in soft peaks. Fold the cream into the
ricotta along with the almond flavouring to
taste.
2. With a sharp knife, cut a cross in each fig at
the stalk end. Continue cutting down almost to
the base of the fig, but keeping the fruit whole.
Gently prise the four 'petals' of each fig apart,
to allow room for the filling.
3. Spoon the ricotta mixture into a piping bag
fitted with a large rosette nozzle. Pipe the
cream into the centre of each fig. Chill until
ready to serve.
4. To serve, arrange fig or vine leaves
decoratively over a flat serving platter. Place
the stuffed figs on top and scatter rose petals
around. Serve well chilled.

Black Fruit Salad

SERVES 4-6

335 g (12 oz) blueberries or blackcurrants
335 g (12 oz) black cherries, stoned
335 g (12 oz) seedless black grapes
finely grated rind and juice of 1 large orange
50-75 g (2-3 oz) light brown soft sugar

1. Mix the fruits together in a bowl with the
orange rind and juice and the sugar. Leave to
stand for 3-4 hours or overnight, stirring
occasionally.

Sparkling Strawberries

SERVES 8

900 g (2 lb) strawberries
1 × 15 ml tbs icing sugar
300 ml (10 fl oz) champagne or sparkling white
   wine, well chilled
Vanilla Wafers (see below) and double cream,
   to serve

1. Rinse the strawberries, and place in a bowl.
Sprinkle icing sugar over and mix in gently.
Chill.
2. Remove the strawberries from the
refrigerator about 30 minutes before serving to
allow to come to room temperature.
3. Just before serving, pour the champagne or
sparkling wine over the top. Serve with wafers
and double cream.

Vanilla Wafers

MAKES 24

75 g (3 oz) butter, softened
75 g (3 oz) caster sugar
few drops of vanilla flavouring
pinch of grated nutmeg
2 egg whites
75 g (3 oz) plain flour

1. Grease 2 baking trays. Cream together the
butter and sugar until very pale and light. Stir
in the vanilla flavouring and nutmeg.
2. Lightly whisk the egg whites and gradually
beat them into the creamed mixture with a
little of the flour. Fold in the remaining flour.
3. Drop heaped teaspoonfuls of the mixture on
to the baking trays, allowing plenty of space to
spread. Bake at 200°C/400°F/Gas Mark 6 for
6-7 minutes, or until set and pale golden
around the edges. Remove from the baking
trays and leave to cool. Store in an air-tight tin.

SPICED FRUIT WAFERS

SERVES 8

175 g (6 oz) caster sugar
300 ml (10 fl oz) water
pared rind and juice of 1 orange
1 cinnamon stick
6 fresh peaches
225 g (8 oz) redcurrants, stalks removed
225 g (8 oz) strawberries, hulled and sliced
300 ml (10 fl oz) double cream
150 ml (5 fl oz) soured cream or Greek-style
    yogurt
24 Vanilla Wafers (see page 18)
icing sugar for dusting
sprigs of redcurrants, strawberries and leaves,
    to decorate

1. Place the caster sugar in a medium saucepan with the water and the pared orange rind and cinnamon stick. Heat gently until the sugar dissolves, stirring. Bring to the boil and bubble for 2 minutes. Remove from the heat.

2. Thickly slice the peaches into the hot syrup, then add the redcurrants. Return to the heat and simmer for 2-3 minutes, or until just tender.

3. With a slotted spoon, transfer the fruit to a bowl. Stir in the strawberries, cover and set aside.

4. Return the liquid in the pan to the heat. Bring to the boil and bubble for 4-5 minutes, or until reduced and syrupy. Strain the orange juice into the pan, then remove from the heat and set aside to cool.

5. Whip the double cream until it just holds its shape. Fold in the soured cream or yogurt. Layer the vanilla wafers with the cream and spiced fruits. Dust the top with icing sugar, decorate with redcurrants, or strawberries and leaves. Serve with the fruit sauce.

Spiced Fruit Wafers

LAYERED FRUIT TERRINE

SERVES 6

2 × 15 ml tbs powdered gelatine
425 ml (15 fl oz) clear grape or apple juice
200 g (7 oz) small black seedless grapes
275 g (10 oz) small even-sized strawberries, hulled
4 large oranges, peeled, segmented and drained
200 g (7 oz) small green seedless grapes
extra strawberries or raspberries, to decorate
SAUCE:
225 g (8 oz) fresh raspberries, hulled, or
   frozen raspberries, thawed
icing sugar, to taste
lemon juice
dash of fruit liqueur or Kirsch (optional)

1. To make the jelly, sprinkle the gelatine over 150 ml (5 fl oz) of the grape juice in a small bowl and leave to soak for 2-3 minutes. Place the bowl over a pan of simmering water and stir until dissolved. Stir the dissolved gelatine into the remaining juice and mix well.
2. Arrange 6 black grapes around the base of a 750 ml (1¼ pt) non-stick loaf tin or mould, then pour in 0.6 cm (¼ in) layer of the jelly. Chill until set.
3. Arrange the whole strawberries in a tightly packed layer over the set jelly. Arrange the black grapes in a thick layer over the strawberries, followed by the oranges, then the green grapes. Make sure the fruit is overlapping or tightly packed.
4. Slowly pour the fruit jelly over the fruit until it just covers the final layer. Tap the mould very lightly on the work surface to remove any air bubbles. Chill for 4 hours or until set.
5. To make the sauce, purée the raspberries in a blender or food processor until smooth. Press through a sieve if liked, and add sugar and lemon juice to taste. Stir in the liqueur, if using. Cover and chill.
6. To serve, dip the tin or mould in a bowl of lukewarm water for about 10 seconds and invert on to a flat surface. Remove the tin and cut the terrine into thick slices. Transfer each slice carefully on to individual chilled plates. Decorate with strawberries and serve with the sauce.

AUTUMN PUDDING

SERVES 4-6

675 g (1½ lb) mixed autumn fruit, such as apples,
   blackberries and plums, prepared
4-6 × 15 ml tbs water
about 25 g (1 oz) soft light brown sugar
8-10 thin slices of day-old bread, crusts removed
double cream, to serve
fresh fruit and fresh mint sprigs, to decorate

1. Stew the fruit gently with the water and the sugar until soft but still retaining their shape. The exact amounts of water and sugar depend on the ripeness and sweetness of the fruit.
2. Meanwhile, cut a round from one slice of bread to neatly fit the bottom of a 1.2 pt pudding basin. Cut 6-8 slices of the bread into fingers about 5 cm (2 in) wide. Put the round at the bottom of the basin and arrange the fingers, overlapping around the sides.
3. When the fruit is cooked, and still hot, pour it gently into the basin, being careful not to disturb the bread framework. Reserve about 3 × 15 ml tbs of the juice. When the basin is full, cut the remaining bread to make a lid and use to cover the fruit.
4. Cover with foil, then a plate or saucer which fits just inside the bowl and put a weight on top. Leave until cool, then chill overnight.
5. To serve, run a round-bladed knife carefully round the edge to loosen, then invert the pudding on to a serving dish. Pour the reserved juice over the top. Serve cold with cream. Decorate with fruit and fresh mint sprigs.

Layered Fruit Terrine

BLUEBERRY OAT CRUMBLE

SERVES 6-8

900 g (2 lb) blueberries, washed
3 × 15 ml tbs light soft brown sugar
2 × 15 ml tbs plain flour
1 × 15 ml tbs lemon juice
custard or single cream, to serve
CRUMBLE TOPPING:
115 g (4 oz) butter, well chilled and diced
115 g (4 oz) plain flour
115 g (4 oz) light soft brown sugar
75 g (3 oz) rolled oats
50 g (2 oz) pecan nuts or walnuts, chopped
   and toasted
grated nutmeg (optional)

1. Mix the blueberries with the sugar, flour and lemon juice in a 1.5 lt (2½ pt) pie dish.
2. To make the crumble topping, rub the butter into the flour in a bowl until the mixture resembles fine breadcrumbs. Stir in the sugar, oats and nuts. Flavour with grated nutmeg, if liked. Spoon the crumble mixture on top of the berries and lightly press down.
3. Bake in the oven at 190°C/375°F/Gas Mark 5 for 30–35 minutes, or until golden brown. Serve warm or cold with custard or cream.

COOK'S TIP You can make this dish when blueberries are readily available in summer and freeze it for a treat in winter. Make in a freezer-proof pie dish, then wrap in freezer foil and freeze for up to 6 months.

BLACKBERRY AND PEAR COBBLER

SERVES 4

450 g (1 lb) blackberries, washed
450 g (1 lb) ripe pears, such as Conference,
   peeled, cored and thickly sliced
finely grated rind and juice of 1 lemon
½ × 5 ml tsp ground cinnamon
TOPPING:
225 g (8 oz) self-raising flour
pinch of salt
50 g (2 oz) butter or margarine, well chilled
   and diced
25 g (1 oz) caster sugar
about 150 ml (5 fl oz) milk, plus extra to glaze

1. Put the blackberries and pears into a
saucepan with the lemon rind and juice and the
cinnamon. Simmer for 15–20 minutes until the
fruit is just tender. Remove from the heat and
leave to cool.
2. To make the topping, place the flour and salt
in a bowl. Rub in the butter until the mixture
resembles fine crumbs. Stir in the sugar.
Gradually add enough milk to make a fairly
soft dough.
3. Roll out the dough on a lightly floured
work surface until 1 cm (½ in) thick. Cut out
rounds using a fluted 5 cm (2 in) pastry cutter.
4. Put the fruit in a pie dish and top with
overlapping pastry rounds, leaving a gap in the
centre. Brush the top of the pastry rounds with
milk. Bake in the oven at 220°C/425°F/Gas
Mark 7 for 10–15 minutes until the pastry is
golden brown. Serve hot.

VARIATION For a tasty wholemeal version,
use 225 g (8 oz) wholemeal flour plus 1 × 5 ml
tsp baking powder instead of self-raising flour
for the topping.

ALMOND APPLE CRUMBLE

SERVES 4

6 crisp eating apples, such as Granny Smiths,
   about 675 g (1½ lb) total weight
1 × 5 ml tsp caster sugar
juice of 1 lemon
8 Amaretti biscuits, about 50 g (2 oz) total weight,
   roughly crumbled
115 g (4 oz) plain flour
25 g (1 oz) soft light brown sugar
½ × 5 ml tsp ground cinnamon
75 g (3 oz) butter, softened
Greek-style yogurt or whipped cream, to serve

1. Peel, core and thickly slice apples. Mix the
apples with the caster sugar and lemon juice in
a 1.2 lt (2 pt) ovenproof dish.
2. To make the crumble topping, mix the
Amaretti biscuit crumbs with the flour, sugar
and ground cinnamon. Rub in the butter until
the mixture is crumbly and just beginning to
hold together.
3. Spoon the topping over the apples. Bake in
the oven at 190°C/375°F/Gas Mark 5 for
about 45 minutes, or until the apples are
tender. (The topping will not change much in
appearance.) Serve warm with Greek-style
yogurt or whipped cream.

VARIATION Use 450 g (1 lb) cooking apples
and 225 g (8 oz) blackberries instead of the
Granny Smiths. Mix with 75 g (3 oz) caster
sugar and the lemon juice.

Blueberry Oat Crumble

PRUNE AND PEAR TORTE SLICE

SERVES 8

225 g (8 oz) no-soak pitted prunes, roughly
   chopped
300 ml (10 fl oz) warm tea
3 × 15 ml tbs lemon juice
450 g (1 lb) ripe dessert pears
25 g (1 oz) fresh white breadcrumbs
50-75 g (2-3 oz) butter, melted
4 large sheets filo pastry – about 24 × 48 cm
   (9½ × 19 in) each
3 × 15 ml tbs apricot preserve
50 g (2 oz) walnut pieces, grilled
icing sugar, to dust

1. Put the prunes in a bowl with the tea and
2 × 15 ml tbs lemon juice. Soak overnight.
2. The next day, strain soaking liquor into a
saucepan. Peel, quarter, core and roughly chop
the pears. Stir into the prunes with the
breadcrumbs and 1 × 15 ml tbs lemon juice.
3. Place one sheet of pastry on the work
surface, brush with melted butter. Continue to
layer up the pastry, buttering each layer.
4. Spoon the filling in a strip along one long
edge of the pastry, leaving 5 cm (2 in) clear at
each end. Fold the ends up over the filling,
buttering the underside of each flap; then roll
up the pastry to enclose the prune mixture. Lift
on to a baking tray and brush with butter.
5. Bake at 200°C/400°F/Gas Mark 6 for
about 30 minutes. Cool for about 20 minutes.
6. Meanwhile, place the apricot preserve in the
saucepan with the soaking liquor. Bubble
down until a syrupy glaze remains, then strain.
7. Brush a little glaze over the torte and
sprinkle over the nuts. Carefully brush with
remaining glaze. Dust with icing sugar. Serve
warm, with crème fraîche or yogurt.

Prune and Pear Torte Slice

BANBURY APPLE PIE

SERVES 6

335 g (12 oz) plain flour, plus extra for dusting
pinch of salt
175 g (6 oz) butter, well chilled and diced
1 × 15 ml tbs caster sugar
1 egg, lightly beaten
675 g (1½ lb) cooking apples
juice of ½ lemon
115 g (4 oz) sultanas
75 g (3 oz) soft light brown sugar
pinch of ground cinnamon
pinch of freshly grated nutmeg
grated rind and juice of 1 orange
fresh milk, to glaze
caster sugar for sprinkling
dairy ice cream, to serve

1. To make the pastry, put the flour and salt in a bowl. Rub in the butter until the mixture resembles fine breadcrumbs. Stir in the caster sugar, then the egg and enough chilled water to bind. Knead lightly on a lightly floured surface, then shape into a ball, wrap in clingfilm and chill for at least 30 minutes.
2. Roll out two-thirds of the pastry on a lightly floured surface and use to line a shallow 900 ml (1½ pt) pie dish.
3. Peel, core and thinly slice the apples. Put in a bowl and sprinkle with lemon juice. Layer the apples, sultanas, brown sugar, spices and orange rind in the pie dish. Sprinkle with the orange juice.
4. Roll out the remaining pastry to form a lid, pressing the edges together. Scallop the edges, then make a slit in the centre of the pie.
5. Brush the top with milk to glaze. Bake in the oven at 200°C/400°F/Gas Mark 6 for 30 minutes until golden brown. Sprinkle the top with caster sugar and serve hot or cold. Accompany with dairy ice cream.

LEMON COCONUT PIE

SERVES 6-8

3 eggs
175 g (6 oz) caster sugar
115 g (4 oz) butter, melted and cooled
115 g (4 oz) flaked almonds
65 g (2½ oz) desiccated coconut
grated rind of 2 lemons
175 ml (6 fl oz) lemon juice
175 ml (6 fl oz) milk
50 g (2 oz) plain flour
icing sugar, to dust

1. Grease and base-line a 21 cm (8½ in) round sandwich tin.
2. Place all the ingredients in a large bowl or food processor and blend for 1 minute. Pour into the tin, levelling the surface.
3. Bake in the oven at 180°C/350°F/Gas Mark 4 for about 1¼ hours, or until golden brown and firm to the touch. Allow to cool in the tin.
4. To serve, turn out on to a serving plate. Dust with icing sugar.

PANADE

SERVES 6-8

175 g (6 oz) butter or margarine
225 g (8 oz) plain flour
a large pinch of ground cinnamon
6 × 15 ml tbs chilled water
675 g (1½ lb) sweet eating apples, peeled,
    cored and grated
675 g (1½ lb) ripe pears, peeled, cored and grated
grated rind and juice of 1 large orange
1 × size 3 egg, beaten, and caster sugar, to glaze

1. Rub 115 (4 oz) butter or margarine into the flour and cinnamon until the mixture resembles breadcrumbs. Add about 6 × 15 ml tbs chilled water, to bind to a soft paste.

2. Roll the dough out thinly and line a 24 cm (9½ in) loose-bottomed fluted flan tin. Re-roll the excess pastry and cut into 1 cm (½ in) wide strips. Cover and refrigerate until required. Bake the flan blind in the oven at 200°C/ 400°F/Gas Mark 6 for about 20 minutes.

3. Meanwhile, melt the remaining butter in a large non-stick frying pan. Stir in the apples and pears, the orange rind and 3 × 15 ml tbs orange juice.

Panade

4. Cook over a high heat, stirring constantly, until all excess moisture has evaporated and the mixture is dry. Spoon into the flan case.

5. Quickly lattice the pastry strips over the fruit mixture. Brush with beaten egg and dust with caster sugar. Bake at 200°C/400°F/Gas Mark 6 for about 20 minutes, or until golden.

27

LEMON AND LIME MERINGUE PIE

SERVES 8

175 g (6 oz) plain flour
150 g (5 oz) butter
275 g (10 oz) caster sugar
3 eggs, separated
1 large lemon
2 limes
5 × 15 ml tbs cornflour
lemon and lime slices, to decorate
single cream, to accompany

1. To make the pastry, put the flour in a bowl. Rub in 115 g (4 oz) well-chilled butter until the mixture resembles fine crumbs. Stir in 25 g (1 oz) caster sugar, then stir in 1 egg yolk beaten with 1-2 × 15 ml tbs chilled water to make a firm dough. Knead lightly, then roll out on a lightly floured surface and use to line a 23 cm (9 in) fluted flan tin. Chill for at least 30 minutes.
2. Bake blind in the oven at 200°C/400°F/Gas Mark 6 for 10-15 minutes, then remove the paper and beans and bake for a further 5 minutes until crisp and golden.
3. Meanwhile, prepare the filling. Finely grate the lemon and lime rinds and place in a saucepan with 3 × 15 ml tbs lemon juice and all the lime juice. Add 300 ml (10 fl oz) water and 75 g (3 oz) of the sugar. Warm gently over a low heat, stirring continuously, until sugar dissolves.
4. Mix the cornflour to a smooth paste with 6 × 15 ml tbs water. Off the heat, stir into the juice, then bring slowly to the boil, stirring all the time. Cook for 1-2 minutes, then cool slightly, then beat in 2 egg yolks and 25 g (1 oz) of the butter. Pour into the prepared pastry shell.
5. Whisk the egg whites until stiff. Whisk in 75 g (3 oz) of the caster sugar until completely

incorporated, then fold in the remaining sugar. Spoon over the lemon and lime filling to cover completely. Rough up the surface of the meringue mixture with a fork.
6. Bake in the oven at 150°C/300°F/Gas Mark 2 for about 35 minutes. The meringue will be soft inside. Serve warm, decorated with lemon and lime slices and cream.

CRUMBLY FRUIT AND NUT PIE

SERVES 6

500 g packet shortcrust pastry
plain flour for dusting
1 egg beaten, to glaze
75 g (3 oz) mixed whole nuts,
   roughly chopped
40 g (1½ oz) butter, chilled and cubed
40 g (1½ oz) demerara sugar
2 × 15 ml tbs plain flour
4 × 15 ml tbs caster sugar
finely grated rind of 1 lemon
½ × 5 ml tsp ground ginger or mixed spice
335 g (12 oz) gooseberries
225 g (8 oz) blackberries, tayberries or
   loganberries, washed

1. Roll out three-quarters of the pastry on a lightly floured surface and use to line a 23 cm (9 in) metal pie plate. Trim the pastry and reserve the trimmings. Chill for at least 30 minutes, then bake the pastry case blind in the oven at 200°C/400°F/Gas Mark 6 for about 10 minutes.
2. To decorate the edge of the pie, roll out pastry trimmings to a thickness of 0.3 cm (⅛ in). Cut into leaf shapes, then place on a baking tray and chill. Brush the edge of the cold baked pastry shell with beaten egg and lay the leaves around the edge to form a wreath. Chill again for at least 15 minutes. Bake in the oven

Crumbly Fruit and Nut Pie

at 190°C/375°F/Gas Mark 5 for 10 minutes, or until lightly coloured.

3. Process the nuts, butter and demerara sugar in a food processor for 10 seconds only.

4. Mix together the flour with the caster sugar, lemon rind and ginger or mixed spice. Sprinkle half the mixture on the bottom of the pie. Toss the remaining flour mixture with the fruit and pile into the pie. Sprinkle with the nut mixture.

5. Bake in the oven at 190°C/375°F/Gas Mark 5 for 15 minutes, until the fruit is lightly cooked, or for 25 minutes if softer fruit is preferred. Serve immediately, accompanied by thin custard, if wished.

29

TART OF MANY FRUITS

SERVES 8

175 g (6 oz) plain flour
pinch of salt
75 g (3 oz) caster sugar
115 g (4 oz) butter, chilled and diced
1 egg, beaten
300 ml (10 fl oz) double cream
500 ml (20 fl oz) fresh custard sauce
selection of fresh fruit in season,
    prepared as necessary
9 × 15 ml tbs apricot conserve
3 × 15 ml tbs orange-flavoured liqueur

1. To make the pastry, sift the flour and salt together on a clean surface. Make a well in the centre of the mixture and add the sugar, butter and egg. Using the fingertips of one hand, pinch and work the sugar, butter and egg together until well blended.

2. Gradually work in all the flour, adding a little water if necessary to bind. Knead lightly until the dough is smooth, then wrap and chill for about 1 hour.

3. Roll out the pastry on a lightly floured surface and use to line a greased 28 cm (11 in) loose-bottomed fluted tart tin. Cover and chill in the refrigerator for at least 30 minutes.

4. Bake the pastry case blind in the oven at 190°C/375°F/Gas Mark 5 for 15–20 minutes, then remove the baking beans and greaseproof paper and bake for a further 10 minutes or until the base is crisp and golden brown. Cool on a wire rack, then remove from the tin and place on a large flat serving plate or platter.

5. Lightly whip the cream and fold into the custard sauce. Fill the pastry case with the mixture. Arrange the fruit on top.

6. To make the glaze, gently heat the apricot conserve with the liqueur. Do not boil. Brush the tart generously with the glaze. Surround with fresh flowers, leaves and fruits.

Tart of Many Fruits

Pear Tart

SERVES 8

175 g (6 oz) plain flour
115 g (4 oz) butter, chilled and diced
25 g (1 oz) caster sugar
1 egg yolk
1 × 15 ml tbs water
7 firm ripe red-skinned pears, about
   1.2 kg (2½ lb) total weight
2 × 15 ml tbs Calvados or brandy
2 × 15 ml tbs lemon juice
8 × 15 ml tbs apricot jam
single cream, to accompany

1. To make the pastry, put the flour in a bowl. Rub in the butter until the mixture resembles fine breadcrumbs. Stir in the sugar and the egg yolk, mixed with the water, to make a firm dough. Knead lightly until just smooth, then roll out the pastry on a lightly floured surface and use to line a 23 cm (9 in) loose-bottomed fluted tart tin.
2. Bake blind in the oven at 200°C/400°F/Gas Mark 6 for 10-15 minutes, then remove the paper and beans and bake for a further 5 minutes until the pastry is crisp and golden brown. Leave to cool.
3. Meanwhile, set aside three of the best pears and peel, quarter and core the remainder. Place in a food processor with 1 × 15 ml tbs each of Calvados and lemon juice. Blend until smooth. Place in a bowl, tightly cover and refrigerate until required – it will discolour slightly.
4. Warm the jam with 1 × 15 ml tbs each of Calvados and lemon juice. Sieve and return to the pan.
5. Spoon the pear purée into the tart shell. Peel, core and thickly slice the remaining pears and scatter them over the purée.
6. Reheat the glaze and then brush it carefully over the pears and spoon it over the pear purée. Leave for 20-30 minutes for the glaze to set before serving the tart with single cream.

Pineapple Tarte Tatin

SERVES 8

50 g (2 oz) caster sugar
175 g (6 oz) butter or margarine, softened
2 egg yolks
115 g (4 oz) self-raising flour
115 g (4 oz) granulated sugar
4 × 15 ml tbs double cream
900 g (2 lb) pineapple, peeled, cored and
   thinly sliced
1 × 15 ml tbs Kirsch (optional)
fresh mint sprigs, to decorate

1. Beat together the caster sugar and 50 g (2 oz) of the butter until pale and light. Beat in the egg yolks, then fold in the flour. Knead lightly together to form a smooth dough. Wrap in clingfilm and chill for 30 minutes.
2. In a small saucepan, slowly heat the remaining butter with the granulated sugar until both have melted, stirring. Bring to the boil, then simmer for 3-4 minutes, beating continuously until smooth, dark and fudge-like. (It may separate, but don't worry.)
3. Take off the heat and leave to cool for 1 minute, then stir in the cream, beating until smooth. If necessary, warm gently, stirring, until completely smooth. Spoon into a shallow 21 cm (8½ in) round, non-stick sandwich tin.
4. Arrange the pineapple in overlapping circles on the fudge mixture. Drizzle the Kirsch over.
5. Roll out the pastry to a 25 cm (10 in) round. Place over the pineapple, tucking and pushing the edges down the side of the tin. Trim off any excess. Stand the tin on a baking tray.
6. Bake in the oven at 200°C/400°F/Gas Mark 6 for about 20 minutes, or until the pastry is a deep golden brown. Run the blade of a knife around the edge of the tin to loosen the pastry. Leave to cool for 2-3 minutes. Turn out on to a flameproof serving dish and place under a hot grill for 2-3 minutes to caramelise the top. Decorate with fresh mint sprigs. Serve hot.

BAKEWELL PUDDING

SERVES 6

213 g packet chilled puff pastry
4 × 15 ml tbs red jam, melted
115 g (4 oz) ground almonds
115 g (4 oz) caster sugar
50 g (2 oz) butter, softened
3 eggs, beaten
¼ × 5 ml tsp almond flavouring
fresh cream or custard, to serve

1. Roll out the pastry on a lightly floured surface and use to line a 900 ml (1½ pt) shallow pie dish. Knock up the edge of the pastry in the pie dish with the back of a knife. Mark the rim with the prongs of a fork.
2. Brush the jam over the pastry base. Chill while making the filling.
3. Meanwhile, beat the almonds with the sugar, butter, eggs and almond flavouring. Pour the filling over the jam, spreading it out evenly. Bake in the oven at 200°C/400°F/Gas Mark 6 for 30 minutes, or until the filling is set. Serve warm or cold, with fresh cream or custard.

LEMON OAT PUDDING

SERVES 6

450 ml (16 fl oz) skimmed milk
175 g (6 oz) porridge oats
75 g (3 oz) caster sugar
25 g (1 oz) butter, diced
finely grated rind and juice of 1 lemon
3 eggs, separated
115 g (4 oz) sultanas

1. Grease a 900 ml (1½ pt) ovenproof serving dish. Place the milk in a heavy-based saucepan and bring to the boil. Add the oats and continue to cook, stirring, for about 3 minutes until the mixture is quite thick.

2. Beat in the sugar, butter, lemon rind and juice. Off the heat, beat in the egg yolks and sultanas.
3. Whisk the egg whites until stiff but not dry. Fold into the oat mixture. Spoon into the ovenproof dish.
4. Bake in the oven at 190°C/375°F/Gas Mark 5 for 30–35 minutes, or until firm and golden. Serve immediately.

BAKED APPLE AND COCONUT PUDDING

SERVES 6

6 medium eating apples, each weighing about
   115 g (4 oz), peeled, cored and sliced
finely grated rind and juice of 1 lemon
115 g (4 oz), plus 2 × 15 ml tbs, soft light
   brown sugar
115 g (4 oz) butter, softened
2 eggs, separated
115 g (4 oz) plain wholemeal flour
1½ × 5 ml tsp baking powder
25 g (1 oz) desiccated coconut
about 4 × 15 ml tbs apricot jam, warmed
shredded coconut, toasted, to decorate
custard, to serve

1. Lightly grease a 24–25 cm (9½–10 in) fluted quiche dish. Place the apples in a large bowl with the lemon juice. Stir in the 2 × 15 ml tbs sugar, making sure the apples are well coated.
2. Gradually beat the 115 g (4 oz) sugar into the butter until well blended. Add the lemon rind, then beat in the egg yolks, one at a time. Stir in the flour, baking powder and desiccated coconut.
3. Whisk the egg whites until stiff but not dry, then fold into the creamed ingredients. Spoon into the quiche dish. Press the apples into the mixture, spooning any juices over them.
4. Stand the dish on a baking tray. Bake at

Baked Apple and Coconut Pudding

160°C/325°F/Gas Mark 3 for 1–1¼ hours, or until well browned and firm to the touch, covering with greaseproof paper if necessary.
5. Cool for about 15 minutes, then brush with the apricot jam and scatter over the toasted shredded coconut. Serve warm with custard.

COOK'S TIP Eating apples are sweeter than cooking apples and many varieties – especially Cox's – hold their shape well when cooked. Juicy slices are baked on top of a light and airy pudding mixture, and a topping of toasted coconut completes the dish.

33

STEAMED OR BAKED PUDDING

SERVES 4

175 g (6 oz) self-raising flour
pinch of salt
75 g (3 oz) shredded beef suet or butter, softened
50 g (2 oz) caster sugar
I egg, beaten
about 6 × 15 ml tbs milk
custard, to serve

1. Grease a 1.2 lt (2 pt) pudding basin if making a steamed pudding, or a deep pie dish if baking.
2. Mix together the flour, salt, suet and sugar. Make a well in the centre and add the egg and enough milk to give a soft dropping consistency. Pour into the prepared dish.
3. If steaming the pudding, cover with pleated greaseproof paper or foil and secure with string. Steam for 1½-2 hours, topping up the pan with boiling water, if necessary.
4. If baking, leave uncovered and bake at 180°C/350°F/Gas Mark 4 for about 1 hour, until well risen. Serve hot with custard.

VARIATIONS

Chocolate Pudding Add 3 × 15 ml tbs cocoa powder, sifted with the flour, or stir 25 g (1 oz) chocolate dots or chips into the basic mixture.

Coconut Pudding Replace 25 g (1 oz) of the flour with 25 g (1 oz) desiccated coconut.

Black Cap Pudding Spoon 3 × 15 ml tbs blackcurrant jam into the bottom of the basin.

Marmalade Pudding Spoon 3 × 15 ml tbs marmalade into the bottom of the basin.

Treacle or Syrup Pudding Spoon 2 × 15 ml tbs treacle or golden syrup into the bottom of the basin.

Lemon or Orange Pudding Add the grated rind of 1 lemon or orange to the mixture.

Castle Puddings Divide lemon pudding mixture between eight dariole moulds, then cover and steam for 30-40 minutes.

Canterbury Pudding Replace half of the flour with fresh breadcrumbs. Add the finely grated rind and juice of 1 lemon and replace half the milk with brandy.

Ginger Pudding Add 1 × 5 ml tsp ground ginger and 25 g (1 oz) chopped stem ginger to the basic mixture. Spoon 2 × 15 ml tbs golden syrup into the bottom of the basin, if liked.

Canary Pudding Replace half of the flour with fresh breadcrumbs. Add the finely grated rind of 1 lemon and 2 × 15 ml tbs Madeira or sweet sherry instead of some of the milk.

College Puddings Replace the flour with 115 g (4 oz) fresh breadcrumbs. Add 115 g (4 oz) mixed sultanas and raisins, ½ × 5 ml tsp baking powder and a large pinch each of ground cinnamon, ground cloves and grated nutmeg. Spoon into six greased dariole moulds, cover with foil and bake in the oven at 180°C/350°F/Gas Mark 4 for 45 minutes.

Eve's Pudding Put 450 g (1 lb) peeled, cored and thickly sliced eating apples in the bottom of a deep pie dish. Make the mixture using butter and bake as above.

COOK'S TIP Any of the puddings can be cooked as individual puddings following the instructions for College Puddings. Decorate with whole or chopped nuts when turned out, if wished.

Clockwise from top left: College Pudding, Lemon Pudding, Treacle Pudding

LIGHT CHRISTMAS PUDDINGS

SERVES 8

225 g (8 oz) sultanas, roughly chopped
150 g (5 oz) raisins, roughly chopped
50 g (2 oz) stoned dates, roughly chopped
50 g (2 oz) currants, roughly chopped
25 g (1 oz) no-soak dried apricots, chopped
1 small eating apple, peeled and grated
finely grated rind of 1 lemon
50 ml (2 fl oz) brandy
115 g (4 oz) butter, softened
115 g (4 oz) soft dark brown sugar
2 × size 3 eggs, beaten
115 g (4 oz) fresh white breadcrumbs
40 g (1½ oz) plain flour
¼ × 5 ml tsp each of grated nutmeg and
   ground cinnamon
½ × 5 ml tsp bicarbonate of soda
frosted holly leaves, to decorate (see Cook's Tip)
brandy sauce, to serve

1. Mix together the dried fruit, apple, rind and
brandy. Cover. Leave in a cool place for 2 days.
2. Beat together the butter and sugar until pale
and fluffy. Beat in the eggs. Add the fruit
mixture with the remaining ingredients. Mix.
3. Divide the mixture between eight 25 cm (10 in)
squares of well-floured muslin. Draw up the edges
and tie with string. Allow room for expansion.
4. Tie the puddings on to skewers and hang them
over a large pan of boiling water. Tightly cover
the pan with foil. Steam for about 1½ hours,
topping up with boiling water, if necessary.
5. While still warm, mould into neat rounds.
Hang in a cool place until dry. Overwrap in
foil and refrigerate for up to a week.
6. To serve, remove foil and steam, as above,
for about 1 hour. Decorate with frosted holly
leaves and serve with brandy sauce.

COOK'S TIP To frost holly leaves, brush with
lemon juice and dust with caster sugar. Place on
non-stick baking parchment until dry.

TRADITIONAL CHRISTMAS PUDDING

SERVES 10

50 g (2 oz) each blanched almonds, pecan and
   brazil nuts, roughly chopped
75 g (3 oz) carrot, peeled and coarsely grated
75 g (3 oz) pitted no-soak prunes, chopped
335 g (12 oz) seedless raisins, currants and
   sultanas, mixed
25 g (1 oz) chopped mixed peel
115 g (4 oz) butter, softened
finely grated rind of 1 lemon
115 g (4 oz) soft dark brown sugar
2 eggs, beaten
50 g (2 oz) fresh brown breadcrumbs
115 g (4 oz) plain wholemeal flour
50 g (2 oz) plain flour
1 × 15 ml tbs ground mixed spice
200 ml (7 fl oz) Guinness
2 × 15 ml tbs brandy
2 × 15 ml tbs black treacle

1. Place the nuts, carrot and prunes in a large
bowl with the mixed dried fruit and peel.
2. Beat the butter and lemon rind until soft.
Gradually beat in the sugar, then the eggs. Stir
into the fruit and nuts. Add all the remaining
ingredients. Cover and leave in a cool place
overnight (not the refrigerator).
3. Grease a 1.5-1.6 lt (2½-2¾ pt) pudding basin.
Beat the pudding mixture well, then spoon
into the prepared basin. Cover with pleated
greaseproof paper or foil and secure with string.
Steam for about 8 hours.
4. Leave to cool, then remove the foil, re-
cover with fresh foil and store for up to 2
months in a cool place.
5. On Christmas day, steam the pudding for
about 5 hours. To serve, uncover and invert on
to a serving plate.

Light Christmas Puddings

RED BERRY FOOL

SERVES 4

1-2 × 15 ml tbs caster sugar
6 × 15 ml tbs water
225 g (8 oz) raspberries
225 g (8 oz) redcurrants
225 g (8 oz) blackcurrants
1 × 15 ml tbs custard powder
1 × 15 ml tbs sugar
300 ml (10 fl oz) milk
150 ml (5 fl oz) whipping cream
mint sprigs, to decorate
crisp biscuits, to serve

1. Put the sugar and water in a saucepan large enough to hold the fruit and heat gently until the sugar dissolves. Reserve a little of each fruit to decorate, then poach the remaining fruit for about 10 minutes, until soft.

2. Remove the pan from the heat. Press the fruit through a sieve into a large bowl, then set aside to cool.

3. Blend the custard powder and sugar with 2 × 15 ml tbs milk. Bring the remaining milk to the boil, then pour on to the mixture, stirring well. Return to a clean saucepan and bring to the boil, stirring continuously. Leave to cool completely.

4. Whip the cream until stiff. Fold the custard and most of the cream into the sieved fruit. Spoon the fool into individual glasses. Pipe each dessert with a rosette of remaining cream and top with the reserved fruit and a mint sprig to decorate. Serve with crisp biscuits.

VARIATION For the more traditional gooseberry fool, use 675 g (1½ lb) gooseberries instead of the berries and currants and add 5-6 × 15 ml tbs caster sugar.

Red Berry Fool

39

Syllabub

SERVES 4

finely grated rind and juice of I lemon
75 g (3 oz) caster sugar
1-2 × 15 ml tbs brandy
2 × 15 ml tbs sweet sherry
300 ml (10 fl oz) double cream
lemon twists, to decorate

1. Soak the lemon rind in the juice for 2–3 hours, then stir in the sugar, brandy and sherry. Stir until the sugar dissolves.
2. Whip the cream lightly until it is just beginning to hold its shape, then gradually add the liquid, whipping continuously. Take care not to over-whip. Spoon into individual glass dishes and serve within 3 hours. Decorate with lemon twists.

COOK'S TIP Syllabubs look best in delicate glass dishes, served with dainty sweet biscuits.

Prune and Port Fool

SERVES 4

115 g (4 oz) pitted prunes, soaked overnight
50 g (2 oz) caster sugar
4 × 15 ml tbs port
finely grated rind and juice of I medium orange
150 ml (5 fl oz) thick custard
150 ml (5 fl oz) double cream
biscuits, to serve

1. Drain the prunes, then put in a saucepan with the sugar, port and orange rind and juice. Simmer for about 15 minutes until soft.
2. Leave to cool slightly, then purée in a blender or food processor. Leave to cool completely.
3. Fold the custard into the puréed prunes. Whip the cream until standing in soft peaks,

then fold into the prune custard until evenly blended.
4. Divide the mixture between four individual glasses. Chill for about 2 hours, or until firm. Serve chilled, with sweet biscuits.

COOK'S TIP Use fresh custard sauce in a carton or canned custard for this recipe.

Boodles Orange Fool

SERVES 6

4-6 trifle sponges, cut into I cm (½ in) thick slices
grated rind and juice of 2 oranges
grated rind and juice of I lemon
25-50 g (1-2 oz) sugar
300 ml (10 fl oz) double cream
orange slices or segments, grated orange rind and
    mint leaves, to decorate

1. Use the sponge slices to line the bottom and halfway up the sides of a deep serving dish or bowl. Mix the orange and lemon rinds and juices with the sugar and stir until the sugar has completely dissolved.
2. In another bowl, whip the cream until it just starts to thicken, then slowly add the sweetened fruit juice, whipping the cream as you do so. Whip until the cream is light and thickened and all the juice absorbed.
3. Pour the mixture over the sponge, cover and chill for at least 2 hours, longer if possible, so the juice soaks into the sponge and the cream thickens. Serve decorated with segments or slices of fresh orange, grated orange rind and mint leaves.

Boodles Orange Fool

BLANCMANGE

SERVES 4

4 × 15 ml tbs cornflour
600 ml (20 fl oz) milk
strip of lemon rind
about 3 × 15 ml tbs sugar

1. Blend the cornflour to a smooth paste with
2 × 15 ml tbs of the milk
2. Put the remaining milk in a saucepan with
the lemon rind, bring to the boil, then strain it
on to the cornflour mixture, stirring well.
3. Return the mixture to the pan and bring to
the boil over a low heat, stirring until the
mixture thickens; cook for a further 3 minutes.
Add sugar to taste.
4. Pour into a 600 ml (20 fl oz) dampened jelly
mould and leave for several hours until set.
Turn out to serve.

VARIATIONS
Chocolate Blancmange Omit the lemon
rind and add 50 g (2 oz) melted chocolate to
the cooked and sweetened mixture.

Coffee Blancmange Omit the lemon rind
and add 1-2 × 15 ml tbs coffee flavouring to
the cooked and sweetened mixture.

Orange Blancmange Substitute 1 × 5 ml
tsp grated orange rind for the lemon rind.

JUNKET

SERVES 4

600 ml (20 fl oz) pasteurised milk (not UHT
    or long-life)
1 × 15 ml tbs caster sugar
2 × 5 ml tsp rennet
freshly ground nutmeg, to serve

1. Gently heat the milk in a saucepan until just
warm to the finger. Remove from the heat and
stir in the sugar until dissolved. Add the rennet,
stirring gently.
2. Pour the mixture into a shallow dish and
leave in a warm place, undisturbed, for 1-1½
hours until the junket has set.
3. Chill in the refrigerator and sprinkle the top
with nutmeg to serve.

STRAWBERRY CUSTARDS

SERVES 6

4 × 5 ml tsp powdered gelatine
3 × 15 ml tbs cold water
600 ml (20 fl oz) fresh custard sauce
675 g (1½ lb) strawberries, hulled
1 × 15 ml tbs icing sugar
a few strawberries, to decorate

1. Sprinkle the gelatine over the cold water
in a heatproof bowl and leave to soften for
1 minute. Place the bowl over a saucepan of
gently simmering water and stir until dissolved.
Cool slightly, then stir the dissolved gelatine
into the custard.
2. Purée the strawberries in a blender or food
processor, then press through a nylon sieve.
Whisk about two-thirds of the purée into the
custard.
3. Pour the custard into six oiled 150 ml
(5 fl oz) ramekins and chill for about 3 hours
or until set.
4. Meanwhile, whisk the icing sugar into the
remaining strawberry purée and chill.
5. To serve, turn out the custards and surround
with the strawberry sauce. Decorate with
strawberries.

Strawberry Custards

CUSTARD CREAM

SERVES 4

2 × 5 ml tsp powdered gelatine
2 × 15 ml tbs cold water
300 ml (10 fl oz) fresh custard sauce
1-2 × 5 ml tsp vanilla flavouring
300 ml (10 fl oz) double cream
sugar to taste

1. In a small heatproof bowl, sprinkle the gelatine over the cold water and leave to soften for 1 minute. Place the bowl over a saucepan of gently simmering water and stir until the gelatine dissolves. Cool slightly, then stir into the custard in a thin, steady stream. Stir in the vanilla flavouring.
2. Whip the cream until stiff, then fold it into the custard. Check the sweetness and add sugar to taste.
3. Pour the custard into a dampened 900 ml (1½ pt) jelly mould and chill for about 3 hours, or until set. Unmould just before serving.

VARIATION Add 50 g (2 oz) preserved ginger, chopped.

CHOCOLATE AND ORANGE TRIFLE

SERVES 8

335 g (12 oz) chocolate sponge cake
4 juicy oranges
8 × 15 ml tbs orange-flavoured liqueur
750 ml (1¼ pt) fresh custard sauce
3 × 15 ml tbs stem ginger syrup
300 ml (10 fl oz) double cream
toasted almonds and stem ginger, to decorate

1. Thinly slice the cake and use it to line the base of a shallow serving dish.

2. Peel and segment the oranges. Arrange the segments on top of the cake. Spoon the liqueur evenly over the cake and orange.
3. In a heavy-based, preferably non-stick, saucepan heat the custard. Stir the ginger syrup into the custard.
4. Pour the custard evenly into the dish over the cake and leave to cool.
5. Whip the cream until it just holds its shape, then spoon on top of the custard. Decorate with almonds and stem ginger.

COOK'S TIP Use bought chocolate cake or use up homemade cake that's past its best.

OLDE ENGLISH TRIFLE

SERVES 6-8

4 trifle sponges
4 × 15 ml tbs cherry jam
15 ratafia biscuits
4 × 15 ml tbs sherry
2 bananas, peeled and sliced
grated rind and juice of ½ lemon
225 g (8 oz) cherries, stoned
750 ml (1¼ pt) fresh custard sauce
150 ml (5 fl oz) double cream
glacé cherries, angelica and 25 g (1 oz) chopped
    nuts, toasted, to decorate

1. Cut the trifle sponges in half and spread with jam, then sandwich together. Arrange in the base of a glass serving dish.
2. Cover with ratafias and sprinkle with sherry. Coat the bananas in lemon juice. Arrange the bananas and cherries on top of the ratafias.
3. Pour the custard over the trifle. Whip the cream until stiff and pipe on the top. Decorate with glacé cherries, angelica and nuts.

Olde English Trifle

MARBLED BLUEBERRY CHEESECAKE

SERVES 6–8

335 g (12 oz) fresh blueberries or blackberries
2 × 15 ml tbs clear honey
115 g (4 oz) crunchy cereal
50 g (2 oz) butter
2 × 250 g tubs mascarpone cheese
300 ml (10 fl oz) double cream
grated rind of 1 orange
50 g (2 oz) icing sugar, sifted
1 × 15 ml tbs powdered gelatine

1. Place 275 g (10 oz) of the blueberries in a saucepan with 3 × 15 ml tbs of the water and 1 × 15 ml tbs of the honey. Cook over a low heat until softened.
2. Place the crunchy cereal in a blender or food processor and process until it looks like coarse crumbs. Melt the butter over a low heat, then stir in the crunchy cereal. Press the mixture into the bottom of a non-stick 20 cm (8 in) spring-release tin. Chill.
3. In a large mixing bowl, put the mascarpone cheese, double cream, orange rind and icing sugar. Beat until smooth, then stir in the remaining honey.
4. Put 4 × 15 ml tbs water into a small bowl and sprinkle the gelatine over it. Leave to soak for 5 minutes until spongy, then place over a pan of simmering water and stir until dissolved. Stir the gelatine into the cheese mixture.
5. Purée the blueberries in a blender or food processor and stir them into the cheese mixture, stirring gently to achieve a marbled look. Pour into the prepared tin and lightly push the remaining blueberries in to the top of the cheesecake. Chill until firm, then carefully remove from the tin.

Marbled Blueberry Cheesecake

SEMOLINA PUDDING

SERVES 4

600 ml (20 fl oz) milk
knob of butter or margarine
4 × 15 ml tbs semolina
50 g (2 oz) sugar

1. Heat the milk and butter in a saucepan until just warm, then sprinkle the semolina over it. Bring to the boil over a low heat, then cook for a further 2-3 minutes, stirring all the time.
2. Remove from the heat and stir the sugar into the mixture. Pour the mixture into a greased ovenproof dish.
3. Bake in the oven at 200°C/400°F/Gas Mark 6 for about 30 minutes, until the pudding is lightly browned.

VARIATION Add the grated rind of 1 orange or lemon to the milk.

RICE PUDDING

SERVES 4

50 g (2 oz) short-grain white rice
2 × 15 ml tbs sugar
600 ml (20 fl oz) milk
knob of butter or margarine
freshly grated nutmeg

1. Grease a 900 ml (1½ pt) ovenproof dish.
2. Add the rice, sugar and milk and stir. Dot with shavings of butter or margarine and sprinkle the nutmeg on top.
3. Bake in the oven at 150°C/300°F/Gas Mark 2 for about 2 hours, stirring after about 30 minutes.

CHOCOLATE VANILLA PUDDINGS

SERVES 8

150 g (5 oz) plain chocolate
150 ml (5 fl oz) double cream
4 eggs
75 g (3 oz) caster sugar
115 g (4 oz) butter, softened and diced
2 × 5 ml tsp vanilla flavouring
75 g (3 oz) fresh white breadcrumbs
single cream, to serve

1. Lightly grease eight 150 ml (5 fl oz) ramekins. Finely chop the chocolate in a food processor. Bring the cream to simmering point. Pour the hot cream on to the chocolate and process until smooth. Cool for 2–3 minutes only.
2. Add 2 whole eggs and 2 yolks, reserving the 2 whites, processing after each addition. Add the sugar, butter and vanilla flavouring. Pour into a bowl and stir in the breadcrumbs.
3. Whisk the reserved egg whites until stiff but not dry. Fold into the chocolate mixture. Pour into the ramekins. Place in a roasting tin and pour in hot water to come halfway up the side of the ramekins.
4. Bake in the oven at 180°C/350°F/Gas Mark 4 for 30–35 minutes, or until set.
5. Cool, then cover and chill overnight. Leave at room temperature for about 45 minutes before serving. Serve with cream.

VARIATION Decorate with chocolate waves: spread about 2 × 15 ml tbs of melted chocolate over the back of a baking tray. Freeze for 1–2 minutes, then allow 20 seconds to bring to room temperature. Push sharp edge of a wallpaper stripping knife, at an angle, into and along the chocolate, moving the blade from left to right to form large waves. Chill to set.

Chocolate Vanilla Puddings

TRIPLE CHOCOLATE BROWNIES

SERVES 8

115 g (4 oz) butter, plus extra for greasing tin
200 g (7 oz) plain chocolate, broken up
150 g (5 oz) white chocolate, roughly chopped
115 g (4 oz) milk chocolate, roughly chopped
115 g (4 oz) walnuts, roughly chopped
2 eggs, beaten
175 g (6 oz) plain flour
vanilla ice cream, to accompany

1. Grease an 18 cm (7 in) square deep cake tin with butter and base-line with non-stick baking parchment.
2. Put the plain chocolate and butter in a heatproof bowl over a pan of gently simmering water. Stir until melted. Allow to cool for about 10 minutes.
3. Stir the white and milk chocolates and the walnuts into the melted chocolate mixture with the eggs. Fold in the flour. Spoon into the prepared tin.
4. Bake in the oven at 180°C/350°F/Gas Mark 4 for 35-40 minutes, or until slightly risen and just firm to the touch. The mixture should still be a little moist in the centre. Cool in the tin for about 10 minutes, then turn out and leave for a further 30 minutes, or until the brownie starts to firm up. Cut into slices and serve warm with vanilla ice cream.

COOK'S TIP To melt chocolate in a microwave, break it up into pieces and place in a bowl. Microwave on MEDIUM for 1-2 minutes.

ALMOND AND HONEY WAFERS

SERVES 6

150 g (5 oz) plain chocolate, broken up
115 g (4 oz) bar white Toblerone
5 × 15 ml tbs double cream
about 150 ml (5 fl oz) soured cream
icing sugar, for dusting
Cape gooseberries, to accompany

1. Line 2 baking trays with non-stick baking parchment. Place the plain chocolate in a heatproof bowl over a pan of gently simmering water. Stir until melted. Spoon half the chocolate at a time into a small paper piping bag fitted with a fine icing nozzle.
2. Pipe thin lines of chocolate to form 12 rough lattice shapes about 8 cm (3 in) wide. Chill for 1 hour to set.
3. Meanwhile, break up the white Toblerone and place with the double cream in a heatproof bowl over a pan of gently simmering water. Stir until melted and combined thoroughly. It will not be completely smooth because of the chopped almonds in the Toblerone. Leave to cool.
4. Stir in the soured cream, cover and chill for about 1 hour.
5. To serve, peel the chocolate lattices off the lining paper and sandwich together with the white chocolate mixture. Keep chilled until serving time. To serve, dust lightly with icing sugar and accompany with Cape gooseberries.

Triple Chocolate Brownies

INDIVIDUAL CHOCOLATE MINT SOUFFLÉS

SERVES 6

a little butter for greasing
150 ml (5 fl oz) milk
12 After Eight mints
25 g (1 oz) butter or margarine
20 g (¾ oz) plain flour
25 g (1 oz) caster sugar
3 eggs, separated

1. Lightly grease six 150 ml (5 fl oz) ramekins. Heat the milk and mints in a pan until evenly blended.
2. Melt the butter in a large heavy-based saucepan. Add the flour and cook for 1 minute, then blend in the milk. Bring to the boil, stirring all the time, and cook the mixture for 1 minute.
3. Cool slightly, then beat in the sugar and egg yolks. Whisk the egg whites until they are stiff but not dry.
4. Beat one spoonful into the sauce to lighten it, then carefully fold in the remaining egg white. Spoon into the prepared dishes. Stand the dishes on a baking tray.
5. Bake in the oven at 190°C/375°F/Gas Mark 5 for 15-20 minutes or until set. Serve straight away.

COOK'S TIP Take care when separating the egg yolks from the whites as even a trace of yolk will prevent the whites from whisking successfully.

For added luxury, pour a little single cream over the top of the soufflés before serving.

STICKY UPSIDE-DOWN PUDDING

SERVES 8

275 g (10 oz) plain chocolate
75 g (3 oz) pecan nuts
115 g (4 oz) butter or margarine
2 eggs
75 g (3 oz) caster sugar
½ × 5 ml tsp vanilla flavouring
1 × 15 ml tbs strong black coffee
75 g (3 oz) self-raising flour
675 g (1½ lb) ripe pears
ice cream, to serve

1. Grease a 1.2 lt (2 pt) round ovenproof dish and line the base with non-stick baking parchment. Roughly chop 75 g (3 oz) of the chocolate and the nuts and set aside.
2. Break up the remaining chocolate and place with the butter in a heatproof bowl over a pan of gently simmering water. Stir until melted, remove from the heat and leave to cool slightly.
3. Beat together the eggs, sugar, vanilla flavouring, coffee and the melted chocolate and nuts and mix well.
4. Peel, quarter and core the pears and arrange them in the prepared dish. Pour the chocolate mixture over the top.
5. Bake in the oven at 190°C/375°F/Gas Mark 5 for 1 hour, covering with foil after 30 minutes. Cool slightly, then turn out on to a plate and serve with ice cream.

Sticky Upside-Down Pudding

HOT CHOCOLATE CHEESECAKE

SERVES 10-12

CHOCOLATE PASTRY:
150 g (5 oz) plain flour
75 g (3 oz) butter, chilled and diced
2 × 15 ml tbs cocoa powder, sifted
2 × 15 ml tbs caster sugar
25 g (1 oz) ground hazelnuts
1 egg yolk
FILLING:
2 eggs, separated
75 g (3 oz) caster sugar
335 g (12 oz) curd cheese
40 g (1½ oz) ground hazelnuts
150 ml (5 fl oz) double cream
25 g (1 oz) cocoa powder, sifted
2 × 5 ml tsp dark rum
icing sugar, for dusting

1. Grease a 20 cm (8 in) round loose-based cake tin.
2. To make the pastry, put the flour in a bowl and rub in the butter until the mixture resembles fine breadcrumbs. Stir in the cocoa powder, sugar and hazelnuts. Add the egg yolk and sufficient water to make a soft dough.
3. Roll out the pastry on a lightly floured surface and use to line the prepared tin. Chill while making the filling.
4. To make the filling, whisk the egg yolks and sugar together in a bowl until thick enough to leave a trail on the surface when the whisk is lifted. Whisk in the cheese, nuts, cream, cocoa powder and rum until blended.
5. Whisk the egg whites until stiff, then fold into the cheese mixture. Pour into the pastry shell and fold the edges of the pastry over the filling.
6. Bake in the oven at 160°C/325°F/Gas Mark 3 for 1½ hours until risen and just firm to the touch. Remove carefully from the tin and dust with icing sugar. Serve while still hot.

CHOCOLATE AND CHESTNUT CREAM VACHERIN

SERVES 8

6 egg whites
335 g (12 oz) caster sugar
75 g (3 oz) hazelnuts, skinned, toasted and
    finely chopped
175 g (6 oz) plain chocolate, broken
500 g (18 oz) sweetened chestnut purée
300 ml (10 fl oz) double cream
a little icing sugar for dusting
whipped cream and cocoa powder, to decorate

1. Line 3 baking trays with non-stick baking parchment. Draw a 20 cm (8 in) circle on each.
2. Whisk the egg whites until stiff but not dry, then gradually whisk in the sugar a little at a time, until the meringue is smooth and shiny. Very lightly fold in the hazelnuts.
3. Either spread the mixture over the marked circles, or use a piping bag with a plain 1 cm (½ in) nozzle to pipe the meringue in a spiral over the circles, starting from the centre.
4. Bake in the oven at 140°C/275°F/Gas Mark 1 for 1-1½ hours, or until dried out. Change the positions of the baking trays during cooking so the meringues dry out evenly. Remove from the oven and leave to cool, then carefully remove the lining papers.
5. Put the chocolate in a heatproof bowl over a pan of gently simmering water. Stir until melted. Soften the chestnut purée in a bowl, then stir in the melted chocolate. Lightly whip the cream until soft peaks form and fold into the chestnut mixture.
6. To assemble the vacherin, sandwich the meringues together with a little of the chestnut cream. Cover the top and sides with the remainder. Decorate with whipped cream and cocoa powder. Chill until ready to serve.

Chocolate and Chestnut Cream Vacherin

CHOCOLATE PECAN PIE

SERVES 6

225 g (8 oz) butter
225 g (8 oz) plain flour
3-4 × 15 ml tbs chilled water
175 g (6 oz) plain chocolate
50 g (2 oz) soft light brown sugar
3 eggs, beaten
175 g (6 oz) pecan nuts or walnuts
clear honey, warmed, to glaze

1. Rub 175 g (6 oz) of butter into the flour until it resembles fine crumbs, then stir in the chilled water to make a dough. Knead until smooth, then roll out on a lightly floured surface and use to line a 34 × 11 cm (13½ × 4½ in) loose-based tranche tin. Bake blind in the oven at 200°C/400°F/Gas Mark 6 for 10-15 minutes, remove the paper and beans and bake for 10-15 minutes until the base is cooked and lightly browned. Cool slightly.
2. Place the chocolate and sugar in a heatproof bowl over a pan of gently simmering water. Stir until smooth. Cool slightly, then stir in the beaten eggs.
3. Scatter 115 g (4 oz) of the nuts into the pastry shell and pour the chocolate mixture over the top.
4. Bake in the oven at 180°C/350°F/Gas Mark 4 for 25-30 minutes or until just set. Cool slightly, then brush with warm honey. Serve warm or cool, topped with the remaining nuts, warmed in a little honey, if wished.

COOK'S TIP Take care when rubbing butter into flour to use only your fingertips. Lift the mixture as you rub and do so quickly and lightly to avoid overworking the mixture.

SQUIDGY CHOCOLATE ROLL

SERVES 6–8

4 × 15 ml tbs cocoa powder
150 ml (5 fl oz) milk
4 eggs, separated
115 g (4 oz) caster sugar
225 ml (8 fl oz) double cream
fresh strawberries and grated chocolate,
    to decorate

1. Grease and line a 20 × 30 cm (8 × 12 in) swiss roll tin. Mix the cocoa powder and milk in a small saucepan and heat gently until the cocoa powder has dissolved. Remove the pan from the heat and set aside to cool.
2. Whisk the egg yolks and sugar together until pale and fluffy. Whisk the cooled milk mixture into the egg yolk mixture.
3. Whisk the egg whites until stiff, then fold into the cocoa mixture. Spread the mixture evenly into the prepared tin and bake in the oven at 180°C/350°F/Gas Mark 4 for about 20 minutes until the sponge has risen and is just firm to the touch.
4. Turn out on to a sheet of greaseproof paper and cover with a warm, damp tea-towel to prevent the sponge from drying out. Leave the sponge to cool for 20 minutes.
5. Meanwhile, whip the cream until stiff. Spread over the sponge, reserving half for decorating and then roll it up carefully. Do not roll it up too tightly and do not worry if it cracks slightly. Pipe the reserved cream on top and decorate with strawberries and grated chocolate. Serve chilled.

Squidgy Chocolate Roll

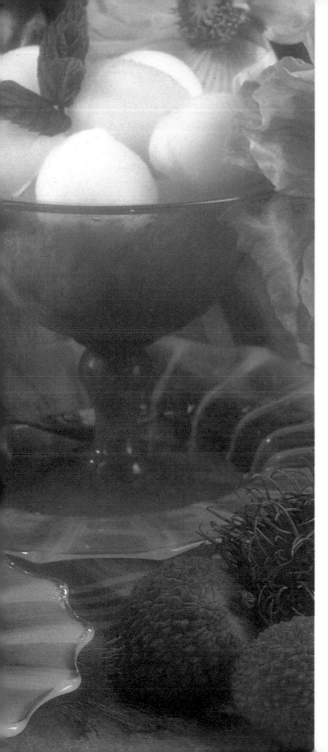

COCONUT ICE CREAM

SERVES 8

275 g (10 oz) sugar
600 ml (20 fl oz) water
1.8 lt (3 pt) coconut milk

1. Place the sugar and water in a saucepan and heat until the sugar dissolves, stirring. Bring to the boil for 10 minutes without stirring. Remove from the heat and leave to cool.
2. Mix the cold syrup with the coconut milk. Pour into a shallow freezerproof container and freeze until mushy, about 3 hours.
3. Place in a chilled bowl and mash to break down the ice crystals. Return the mixture to the container and freeze for a further 2 hours, or until mushy. Mash as before, then return to the freezer for at least 3 hours.
4. Soften at room temperature for 20–30 minutes. Serve with Ginger Thins (see below).

GINGER THINS

MAKES ABOUT 35

175 g (6 oz) plain flour
pinch of salt
¾ × 5 ml tsp ground ginger
115 g (4 oz) butter, chilled and diced
50 g (2 oz) caster sugar, plus extra for dusting

1. Line a baking tray with greaseproof paper. Sift together the flour, salt and ginger. Rub in the butter. Stir in the sugar and knead.
2. Roll out the dough 0.3 cm (⅛ in) thick and stamp into 5 cm (2 in) rounds. Transfer to the lined baking tray and chill for 20 minutes.
3. Bake in the oven at 180°C/350°F/Gas Mark 4 for 15 minutes. Dredge with caster sugar while still warm. Cool on a wire rack.

Coconut Ice Cream

BRANDY ICE CREAM WITH RAISIN CREAM SHERRY

SERVES 8

150 g (5 oz) raisins, finely chopped
150 ml (5 fl oz) cream sherry
300 ml (10 fl oz) double cream, lightly whipped
75 ml (3 fl oz) brandy
50 g (2 oz) caster sugar
2 × 500 g cartons fresh custard sauce

1. Soak the raisins in the sherry. Cover and leave overnight.

2. Stir the cream, brandy and sugar into the custard.

3. Pour into a freezerproof container to a depth of about 4 cm (1½ in). Freeze until it starts to freeze around the edge, about 2 hours, then stir. Freeze again for about 1½ hours. Stir gently, then freeze until firm, about 8 hours.

4. Transfer the ice cream to the refrigerator to soften 30 minutes before serving. Serve in scoops with the raisin, cream sherry served separately. Accompany with sweet biscuits.

Brandy Ice Cream with Raisin Cream Sherry

KULFI

SERVES 8

1.8 lt (3 pts) milk
6 green cardamom pods
150 g (5 oz) sugar
50 g (2 oz) ground almonds
25 g (1 oz) pistachio nuts, blanched and chopped
150 ml (5 fl oz) double cream
shredded pistachio nuts, to decorate

1. Put the milk and cardamom pods in a large heavy-based saucepan and bring to the boil. Simmer for about 1 hour, or until the milk has reduced by half, stirring occasionally.
2. Add the sugar, stirring well until dissolved. Strain the milk into a bowl and stir in the ground almonds. Leave to cool.
3. Stir the pistachio nuts and cream into the cold milk mixture.
4. Pour into a shallow freezerproof container and freeze for about 3 hours until just mushy.
5. Place in a chilled bowl and beat. Work quickly so that the ice cream does not melt completely.
6. Return the mixture to the container and freeze again for about 1 hour until mushy. Beat again, then spoon into eight kulfi moulds or ramekins. Cover and freeze.
7. Transfer to the refrigerator to soften 30 minutes before serving. Unmould and decorate.

BROWN BREAD ICE CREAM

SERVES 4

115 g (4 oz) fresh wholemeal breadcrumbs
75 g (3 oz) light muscovado sugar
150 ml (5 fl oz) whipping cream
300 ml (10 fl oz) low-fat natural yogurt

1. Mix the breadcrumbs with 50 g (2 oz) of the sugar and spread on a baking sheet. Bake in the oven at 200°C/400°F/Gas Mark 6 for 10–15 minutes, turning occasionally, until crisp and lightly browned. Alternatively, toast under the grill, turning frequently to prevent burning. Set aside to cool, then break up.
2. Whip the cream until thick, then stir in the yogurt and remaining sugar. Stir in the toasted breadcrumbs, reserving 25 g (1 oz) for the topping.
3. Pour into a freezerproof container and freeze for 4 hours until firm. Transfer to the refrigerator to soften 30 minutes before serving. To serve, scoop into serving dishes and sprinkle with the reserved crumbs.

FROZEN CHRISTMAS PUDDING

SERVES 8

50 g (2 oz) no-soak dried apricots, chopped
175 g (6 oz) mixed currants, raisins and sultanas
finely grated rind of 1 orange
finely grated rind of 1 lemon
4 × 15 ml tbs rum or brandy
1 × 5 ml tsp ground mixed spice
300 ml (10 fl oz) double cream
500 g carton fresh custard sauce
75 g (3 oz) caster sugar
brandy, to serve (optional)

1. Mix the apricots and dried fruits with the orange and lemon rinds, the rum and mixed spice. Cover and leave to soak for at least 15 minutes.
2. Whisk the cream until it just holds its shape, then fold into the fruit with the custard and sugar.
3. Pour the mixture into a freezerproof container and freeze for about 2 hours. Stir gently to distribute the fruits and break down any ice crystals. Freeze again for at least 6 hours, until firm.
4. To serve, leave at room temperature for 15 minutes. Serve in scoops with a little brandy poured over each portion, if wished.

LIME AND CRANBERRY ICE CREAM

SERVES 8

565 g (1¼ lb) fresh cranberries
750 ml (25 fl oz) fresh custard sauce
500 g pot bio natural yogurt
grated rind and juice of 2 limes
50 g (2 oz) sugar
juice of 1 orange

1. Put 335 g (12 oz) of the cranberries in a saucepan with 1-2 × 15 ml tbs water (just enough to stop the cranberries sticking to the pan) and cook over a gentle heat to soften them slightly, then drain them.
2. Put the custard in a bowl. Stir in the yogurt, the softened cranberries, lime rind and 2 × 15 ml tbs lime juice. Blend in batches in a food processor until almost smooth.
3. Pour into a freezerproof container to a depth of about 5 cm (2 in). Freeze until mushy, about 4 hours, then beat well to break down ice crystals. Freeze again until firm, at least 8 hours. (If using an ice-cream maker, churn mixture according to the manufacturer's directions.)
4. Place remaining cranberries in a pan with the sugar and orange juice. Place over a gentle heat, stirring, until sugar dissolves and the cranberries soften slightly. Pour into a bowl and leave to cool. Cover and chill.
5. About 30 minutes before serving, transfer ice cream to the refrigerator to soften. Serve in scoops with the cranberries in syrup.

MELON ICE

SERVES 6-8

450 ml (16 fl oz) double cream
75 g (3 oz) caster sugar
675 g (1½ lb) ripe orange-fleshed melon, such as charentais or cantaloupe, halved and seeded
250 ml (9 fl oz) sweet wine, such as Moscatel de Valencia, or a light sugar syrup
1 ripe ogen or galia melon, halved and seeded
Ginger Thins (see page 59), to serve
fresh mint sprigs, to decorate

1. Gently heat the cream and sugar until the sugar dissolves, stirring, then set aside to cool.
2. Place the melon flesh in a food processor with half the wine. Blend until smooth, then sieve to remove any coarse fibres.
3. Mix the sweetened cream with the purée. Pour into a freezerproof container. Freeze for 2½-3 hours, then stir to break down any ice crystals. Repeat this process twice, then leave to freeze for at least 2 hours until firm.
4. Scoop out the ogen or galia melon flesh with a melon baller and place in serving bowls. Pour 2 × 15 ml tbs of the remaining wine over each serving. Marinate in the refrigerator for about 1 hour.
5. To serve, scoop the melon ice into balls and serve with the marinated melon and Ginger Thins. Decorate with mint sprigs.

COOK'S TIP Although any freezerproof container is suitable for holding water ices or ice creams, a shallow one speeds up the freezing process.

Melon Ice

CHARENTAIS GRANITA

SERVES 4

1.6 kg (3½ lb) charentais melon, peeled,
    seeded and cut into chunks
1 × 15 ml tbs clear light honey such as Acacia
finely grated rind and juice of 1 small orange
finely grated rind and juice of 1 lemon
fresh mint sprigs, to decorate

1. Purée the melon in a blender or food
processor. Put in a bowl with the honey, rinds
and juices and mix well.
2. Transfer to a freezer container and freeze for
3 hours, or until ice crystals begin to form
around the edges.
3. Place in a chilled bowl and beat until
smooth. Return to the container and freeze for
about 4 hours, or until frozen. To serve, place
in the refrigerator for about 45 minutes to
soften. Spoon into chilled glasses or dishes and
decorate with mint sprigs.

ORANGE WATER ICE

SERVES 6

175 g (6 oz) sugar
425 ml (15 fl oz) water
10 large oranges
finely pared rind and juice of 1½ lemons

1. Put the sugar in a pan with the water. Heat
gently until the sugar dissolves, stirring. Bring
to the boil and boil gently for 10 minutes
without stirring.
2. Meanwhile, thinly pare off the rind from 4
of the oranges and the lemons.
3. Add the orange and lemon rinds to the sugar
syrup and leave to go quite cold.
4. Squeeze the juice from the 4 oranges and the
lemons. Strain into a measuring jug – there
should be 425 ml (15 fl oz).

5. Strain the cold syrup into a shallow
freezerproof container and stir in the fruit
juices. Mix well, then freeze for about 4 hours
until mushy.
6. Place the mixture in a chilled bowl and beat
with a fork to break down the ice crystals.
Return to the freezer and freeze until firm, at
least 4 hours.
7. Meanwhile, using a serrated knife, cut away
the peel and pith from the remaining oranges.
Slice the oranges into thin rings and discard any
pips. Place the oranges in a serving bowl.
Cover tightly with clingfilm and refrigerate
until serving time.
8. To serve, place the water ice in the
refrigerator for 45 minutes to soften. Serve
with the fresh orange slices.

COOK'S TIP Serve this tangy water ice for a
dinner party dessert after a rich or substantial
main course. It is particularly refreshing after a
spicy curry.

VARIATIONS
Lemon Water Ice With 6–8 lemons as a
basis, follow the recipe using the pared rind of
4 lemons and enough juice to give 425 ml
(15 fl oz).

Strawberry Water Ice With 675 g (1½ lb)
strawberries, puréed and sieved, and the pared
rind and juice of 1 orange as a basis, follow the
recipe, using the strawberry purée and orange
juice instead of the orange and lemon juices in
step 4.

Coffee Water Ice Put 2 × 15 ml tbs sugar
and 50 g (2 oz) finely ground Italian coffee in a
jug, pour in 600 ml (20 fl oz) boiling water and
leave to stand for 1 hour. Strain the coffee
through a filter paper or muslin, then follow
the recipe after the straining in step 5.

*Clockwise from top right: Strawberry Water Ice,
Lemon Water Ice, Orange Water Ice*

MANGO AND CARDAMOM GÂTEAU

SERVES 10

seeds from 4 green cardamom pods
good pinch of saffron strands
I quantity Genoese Sponge mixture
(see page 70)
FILLING AND DECORATION:
150 ml (5 fl oz) double cream
150 ml (5 fl oz) Greek-style yogurt
3 × 15 ml tbs icing sugar
2 large ripe mangoes, peeled and sliced
4 × 15 ml tbs orange juice
icing sugar for dusting
grated rind, to decorate

I. Crush the cardamom seeds and saffron strands to a powder. Prepare the Genoese Sponge, sifting the spices with the flour.
2. Whip the cream until it holds its shape. Stir the yogurt in with 2 × 15 ml tbs icing sugar. Sandwich the sponge with the cream mixture and half the sliced mango, then chill for 2–3 hours.
3. Meanwhile, purée the remaining mango with 1 × 15 ml tbs icing sugar and the orange juice. Rub through a sieve to remove any fibres. Cover and chill.
4. Dust the gâteau with icing sugar and decorate with grated orange rind just before serving. Serve with the mango sauce.

COOK'S TIP Mangoes are a wonderfully exotic fruit with a deliciously tropical flavour. To test if a mango is ripe, squeeze it gently – it should feel really soft.

Mango and Cardamom Gâteau

RED FRUIT GÂTEAU

SERVES 10

SAUCE:

**675 g (1½ lb) mixed red summer fruit,
such as raspberries, strawberries,
redcurrants, loganberries, prepared**

sugar, to taste

3 × 15 ml tbs lemon juice

1-2 × 15 ml tbs water

1 Genoese Sponge (see page 70)

450 g (1 lb) mixed summer fruit, prepared

300-450 ml (10-16 fl oz) double cream

frosted fruits and flowers, to decorate

1. To make the sauce, put the fruit, sugar and lemon juice into a pan and heat gently until the juice starts to run from the fruit and the sugar melts. Add the water and press through a nylon sieve, or purée and then sieve. Chill until ready to serve.

2. Cut the cake into two layers and sandwich together with some of the fruit sauce and the prepared fruit. Whip the cream until it holds its shape and spread it evenly over the top and sides of the cake. Decorate with frosted fruits and flowers. Serve the remaining sauce separately.

Red Fruit Gâteau

ALMOND CREAM GÂTEAU

SERVES 8

290 g (10½ oz) plain flour, plus extra for dusting
75 g (3 oz) ground almonds
175 g (6 oz) butter, softened, plus extra for
   greasing
150 g (5 oz) caster sugar
5 whole eggs
1 egg yolk
few drops of vanilla flavouring
few drops of almond flavouring
25 g (1 oz) cornflour, sifted
450 ml (16 fl oz) milk
300 ml (10 fl oz) double cream
115 g (4 oz) granulated sugar
icing sugar, fresh strawberries and strawberry
   leaves, to decorate

1. To make the almond pastry, sift 175 g (6 oz) of the flour into a bowl. Make a small well in the centre and sprinkle in the almonds. Place 75 g (3 oz) of the butter, 75 g (3 oz) of the caster sugar, 1 egg, 1 egg yolk and the vanilla flavouring in the centre and blend well with the fingertips.

2. Draw the flour and almonds into the butter mixture and knead together lightly until smooth. Wrap and chill for about 30 minutes.

3. To make choux pastry, place the remaining butter in a saucepan with 200 ml (7 fl oz) water. Melt the butter over a low heat, stirring, then bring the water to the boil. Off the heat, tip in 90 g (3½ oz) of the flour. Beat until smooth. Cool before gradually beating in 3 eggs.

4. Using a 1 cm (½ in) plain nozzle, pipe 24 rounds of choux pastry on to a greased and dampened baking sheet. Bake in the oven at 200°C/400°F/Gas Mark 6 for 20-25 minutes until well risen and golden. Split each round horizontally with a knife and return to the oven for 5-10 minutes to dry out. Cool on a wire rack.

5. Roll out the almond pastry on a lightly floured surface into a circle with a 28 cm (11 in) diameter and use to line the base and sides of a 23 cm (9 in) deep fluted flan ring. Freeze for 15 minutes. Bake blind in the oven at 200°C/400°F/Gas Mark 6 for 20 minutes, then remove the beans and paper and bake for a further 5-10 minutes, or until the base is golden brown and cooked through. Cool.

6. To make the custard, whisk the remaining caster sugar with the remaining flour, the remaining egg, almond flavouring and cornflour. Put the milk in a saucepan and bring to the boil. Pour on to the flour mixture, whisking all the time. Return the mixture to the clean pan, bring to the boil, boil for 1 minute, then lower the heat and simmer gently for 2–3 minutes, stirring all the time, until smooth and thick. Spoon into a heatproof bowl and cover with damp greaseproof paper. Cool.

7. Lightly whisk the double cream until it just begins to hold its shape. Fold into the cold custard mixture, whisking lightly together if necessary. Fill the choux rounds with about half the mixture. Spoon the remainder into the cold flan case. Pile the choux rounds on top of the custard. Chill.

8. To make the caramel sauce, melt the granulated sugar slowly over a gentle heat in a heavy-based saucepan. When it is dissolved and golden brown, remove it from the heat and drizzle over the choux buns. Decorate with icing sugar, strawberries and leaves.

ALMOND TORTE

SERVES 8-10

115 g (4 oz) butter, softened
115 g (4 oz) caster sugar
finely grated rind of 1 orange
2 eggs, beaten
115 g (4 oz) ground almonds
175 g (6 oz) semolina
2 × 5 ml tsp baking powder
1 × 5 ml tsp almond flavouring
2 × 15 ml tbs orange juice
GRAND MARNIER SYRUP:
75 g (3 oz) sugar
200 ml (7 fl oz) water
4 × 15 ml tsp **Grand Marnier**
toasted ground almonds and icing sugar,
    to decorate

1. Grease and base-line a sloping-sided cake tin, about 5 cm (2 in) deep and 21 cm (8½ in) across the base, or a deep, round cake tin with non-stick baking parchment.
2. Beat the butter, the sugar and orange rind until pale and light. Gradually beat in the eggs.
3. Beat in the almonds, semolina, baking powder, almond flavouring and orange juice until evenly blended. Pour into the tin, and level the surface with the back of a spoon.
4. Bake at 220°C/425°F/Gas Mark 7 for 10 minutes, then at 180°C/350°F/Gas Mark 4 for a further 25 minutes, or until well browned and firm to the touch. A skewer inserted into the centre should come out clean.
5. Meanwhile, make a Grand Marnier Syrup. Put the sugar in a pan with 200 ml (7 fl oz) water and the Grand Marnier. Heat gently until the sugar dissolves, stirring. Bring to the boil, then simmer for 1 minute.
6. Cool the torte in the tin for 10-15 minutes, then turn out on to a plate. Carefully spoon over the Grand Marnier Syrup. Leave to cool.
7. To serve, sprinkle with the almonds and sifted icing sugar. Cut into thin wedges.

GENOESE SPONGE

SERVES 10

50 g (2 oz) unsalted butter, cut into small cubes
4 eggs
115 g (4 oz) caster sugar
90 g (3½ oz) plain flour

1. Grease a 21 cm (8½ in) moule à manque or spring-release tin and line with non-stick baking parchment.
2. Put the butter in a small bowl and stand in a pan containing about 2.5 cm (1 in) hot water; stir occasionally until it melts. Cool slightly.
3. Place the eggs and sugar in a large bowl and whisk until thick and mousse-like, about 10 minutes. Sift half the flour over the egg mixture and fold in with a metal spoon. Gently pour the butter around the edge of the mixture, then sift the remaining flour over. Fold the butter and flour into the egg mixture. Pour into the tin and smooth over the surface.
4. Bake in the oven at 180°C/350°F/Gas Mark 4 for about 40 minutes until well risen and firm to the touch. Turn out on to a wire rack and leave to cool. Carefully split into two discs with a large serrated knife.

COOK'S TIP You can't beat a light-as-a-feather sponge to create a mouthwatering dessert. Lots of gâteaux are based on a Genoese sponge. It is delicious enough simply to split and fill with fruit and cream, or it can be transformed into totally irresistible, decadent desserts with nuts and liqueurs.

It is important to add the butter slowly, carefully and lightly in step 3 or the cake will have a heavy texture.

Almond Torte

Apple and Pecan Meringue Cake

SERVES 12

115 g (4 oz) caster sugar
175 g (6 oz) soft light muscovado sugar
4 egg whites
115 g (4 oz) pecan nuts, roughly chopped
2 x 5 ml tsp ground cinnamon
675 g (1½ lb) cooking apples
1 lemon
50 ml (2 fl oz) water
450 g (1 lb) eating apples
50 g (2 oz) butter
300 ml (10 fl oz) double cream
150 ml (5 fl oz) fromage frais
icing sugar and cinnamon to dust

1. Line two baking trays with non-stick baking parchment and draw a 28 cm (11 in) diameter circle on each. Turn the paper over so that the pencil mark is underneath. Sieve together the caster sugar and 115 g (4 oz) muscovado sugar.
2. Whisk the egg whites until stiff but not dry. Gradually whisk in the mixed sugars, 1 × 15 ml tbs at a time. Gently fold in three-quarters of the chopped nuts and the cinnamon.
3. Using two dessert spoons, shape the meringue into ovals; arrange about 16 in a round. Sprinkle with remaining chopped nuts. Spread the remaining meringue into a round on the second baking tray.
4. Bake in the oven at 150°C/300°F/Gas Mark 2 for 1½ -2 hours or until firm. When cold, peel off the baking parchment.
5. Meanwhile, peel, quarter, core and roughly chop the cooking apples. Place in a saucepan with grated rind and juice of the lemon and the water. Slowly bring to the boil and simmer until the apple softens; cool.
6. Peel, core and cut the eating apples into 0.6 cm (¼ in) thick slices. Melt the butter in a frying pan over a low heat. Stir in 50 g (2 oz)

muscovado sugar. Increase the heat slightly and sauté the apple slices until they caramelise. Remove the apple and cool on lightly oiled foil. Take the remaining caramel off the heat.
7. To assemble, spoon the apple purée over the flat base. Lightly whisk the cream until it just holds its shape, fold in the fromage frais. Spoon over the purée. Place the meringue ring on top and fill the centre with caramelised apple slices, spooning over any remaining caramel. Dust with icing sugar and cinnamon.

Red Berry Vacherin

SERVES 6

4 egg whites
225 g (8 oz) caster sugar
300 ml (10 fl oz) double cream
115 g (4 oz) strawberries, halved
115 g (4 oz) raspberries
115 g (4 oz) redcurrants, stripped from stalks

1. Draw a 20 cm (8 in) circle on non-stick baking parchment and place on a baking tray.
2. Put the egg whites in a large bowl and whisk until very stiff, then whisk in half the sugar. Fold in the remaining sugar.
3. Spoon half the mixture into a piping bag fitted with large star nozzle and pipe the mixture on to the circle, starting from the centre.
4. Using the remaining meringue mixture, pipe rosettes on to the meringue base.
5. Bake at 130°C/250°F/Gas Mark ½ for 2 hours or until dry and crisp but still white. Ease the meringue off the paper. Leave to cool.
6. To serve, whip the cream until standing in soft peaks. Spread in the middle of the meringue base. Arrange the strawberries in a circle around the edge of the centre, then the raspberries. Pile the redcurrants in the centre. Serve at once.

Apple and Pecan Meringue Cake

GOLDEN MASCARPONE TARTS WITH PEAR SAUCE

SERVES 10

275 g (10 oz) plain flour
175 g (6 oz) caster sugar
150 g (5 oz) unsalted butter, chilled and diced
4-5 × 15 ml tbs water
450 g (1 lb) pears
2 bananas
335 g (12 oz) fresh dates
40 g (1½ oz) butter
335 g (12 oz) mascarpone cheese
300 ml (10 fl oz) double cream
2 × 15 ml tbs rum
½ × 5 ml tsp vanilla flavouring
8 × 15 ml tbs soft dark brown sugar
PEAR SAUCE:
115 g (4 oz) caster sugar
grated rind and juice of 1 lemon
350 ml (12 fl oz) water
450 g (1 lb) ripe pears

1. Put the flour and 115 g (4 oz) of the caster sugar in a bowl. Rub in the unsalted butter until the mixture resembles breadcrumbs, then add enough water to bind. Gently knead until smooth. Wrap and chill for 30 minutes.
2. Roll out the dough on a lightly floured surface and use to line two 34 × 11 cm (13½ × 4½ in) loose-based, fluted tart tins. Bake blind in the oven at 200°C/400°F/Gas Mark 4 for 10-15 minutes, then remove the paper and beans and bake 10-15 minutes longer, until crisp and golden. Leave to cool.
3. Peel, quarter and core the pears. Slice the bananas. Halve and stone the dates. Melt the butter in a large, heavy-based frying pan. Stir in the pears and dates and cook gently, stirring, for 3-4 minutes until beginning to soften. Add the bananas and cook for a further minute.
4. Divide the fruit between the tart tins. Leave to cool. Whisk together the next four

ingredients with the remaining caster sugar until smooth. Spoon the mixture over the fruit to cover it. Chill.
5. Sprinkle 4 × 15 ml tbs dark brown sugar over each tin. Place under a hot grill to caramelise the sugar. Leave to cool, then chill.
6. Meanwhile, make the pear sauce. Place the sugar in a pan with the lemon rind and water. Heat gently until the sugar dissolves. Bring to the boil, then simmer for 1 minute.
7. Peel, quarter, core and roughly chop the pears. Add to the sugar syrup. Bring to the boil, then simmer gently for about 5 minutes, or until just softened.
8. Blend in a food processor, then sieve and stir in 1 × 15 ml tbs lemon juice. Leave to cool.
9. Serve the tarts, cut into slices, accompanied by the pear sauce.

CARAMELISED APPLE WAFERS WITH CUSTARD

SERVES 6

500 g packet chilled puff pastry
flour for dusting
1 egg, beaten, to glaze
icing sugar for dusting
175 g (6 oz) white marzipan
2 small Granny Smith apples
25 g (1 oz) butter, melted
3 × 15 ml tbs caster sugar
fresh custard sauce, to serve
ground cinnamon for dusting

1. Draw a heart-shaped template 10 cm (4 in) across at its widest point and the same lengthways and cut out. Draw a second heart-shaped template 2.5 cm (1 in) smaller all round and cut out.

Caramelised Apple Wafers with Custard

2. Roll out the pastry on a lightly floured surface to a 30 cm (12 in) square. Cut out 6 hearts, using the larger template. Place on a wetted baking sheet and brush with the beaten egg.

3. Dust icing sugar on to the work surface and roll out the marzipan to about 0.5 cm (¼ in) thick. Cut out 6 hearts, using the smaller template. Place these on top of the pastry hearts already on the baking sheet.

4. Peel, quarter and core the apples. Cut each quarter into 3 or 4 slices and arrange on the marzipan in a fan shape. Brush with melted butter and sprinkle with the caster sugar.

5. Bake in the oven at 220°C/425°F/Gas Mark 7 for about 15 minutes until the pastry is golden and the apples are beginning to caramelise. Serve warm, dusted with icing sugar and accompanied by the custard, lightly dusted with cinnamon.

SUMMER PROFITEROLES

SERVES 8

CHOUX BUNS:
50 g (2 oz) butter
150 ml (5 fl oz) water
65 g (2½ oz) strong plain flour
pinch of salt
2 eggs, lightly beaten
CHOCOLATE SAUCE:
225 g (8 oz) caster sugar
300 ml (10 fl oz) water
115 g (4 oz) cocoa powder
FILLING:
350 ml (12 fl oz) double cream, whipped
225 g (8 oz) strawberries, hulled and sliced

1. Prepare the choux buns. Grease a baking sheet. In a pan, heat the butter and water until the butter has melted, then bring to the boil.
2. Take the pan off the heat and quickly stir in the sifted flour and salt. Return the pan to the heat and stir until the mixture forms a ball in the centre.
3. Allow the mixture to cool before adding the eggs, a little at a time, beating thoroughly.
4. Using a piping bag and wide nozzle, pipe 8 equal rounds of dough on to the baking sheet.
5. Bake in the oven at 220°C/425°F/Gas Mark 7 for 15–20 minutes.
6. Transfer the buns to a wire rack to cool.
7. Prepare the chocolate sauce. Place the sugar and water in a pan together. Stir over a low heat until the sugar dissolves, then bring the liquid to the boil and simmer for 1 minute.
8. Whisk the cocoa powder into the sugar liquid until smooth. Bring to the boil, then turn off the heat and leave to cool.
9. Cut the choux buns in half and fill the base with the whipped cream and strawberries.
10. Dip the bun top in chocolate sauce, then place over the strawberries and cream.

LEMON GINGER CHEESECAKE

SERVES 8

115 g (4 oz) digestive biscuits, finely crushed
25 g (1 oz) stem ginger, finely chopped
50 g (2 oz) butter, melted
225 g (8 oz) full-fat soft cheese
405 g can condensed milk
175 ml (6 fl oz) lemon juice
whipped cream and caramel shapes (see Cook's Tip), to decorate

1. Line the base and sides of a 20 cm (8 in) spring–release cake tin with non–stick baking parchment.
2. Mix the biscuits and ginger together with the butter. Press across the base and halfway up the sides of the tin, then refrigerate until set, about 30 minutes.
3. In a food processor or blender, blend the cheese and the condensed milk until smooth. Gradually drizzle in the lemon juice and continue blending for a further 2 minutes.
4. Pour the mixture over the set base and smooth the surface. Cover and return to the fridge for at least 3 hours to set.
5. To serve, remove from tin and decorate with whipped cream and caramel shapes.

COOK'S TIP To make caramel shapes, place 75 g (3 oz) granulated sugar in a small saucepan. Heat gently until sugar has dissolved, stirring all the time. Increase the heat until the syrup turns a golden caramel colour. Drizzle caramel from the end of a fork on to lightly oiled foil in irregular shapes. Leave the shapes to set at room temperature.

EASTER CHEESECAKE

SERVES 8

225 g (8 oz) plain flour
90 g (3½ oz) caster sugar
115 g (4 oz) butter, diced
4 × 15 ml tbs water
400 g (14 oz) full-fat soft cheese
2 eggs, separated
½ × 5 ml tsp vanilla flavouring
200 ml (7 fl oz) double cream
150 ml (5 fl oz) soured cream
1 ripe pear
icing sugar for dusting
sugared flowers, to decorate

1. Put the flour and 40 g (1½ oz) of the caster sugar into a bowl. Rub in the butter until the mixture resembles fine breadcrumbs, then add the water, to bind.
2. Roll out the pastry on a lightly floured surface and use to line a 21 cm (8½ in) fluted, deep loose-bottomed tart tin. Chill for 15 minutes. Bake blind in the oven at 200°C/400°F/Gas Mark 6 for 20-25 minutes, then remove the paper and beans and bake for a further 10-15 minutes until the base is crisp and golden.
3. Beat together the soft cheese, egg yolks and vanilla flavouring. Gradually beat in the creams.
4. Whisk the egg whites until they just hold their shape. Fold in 25 g (1 oz) of caster sugar and continue whisking until stiff. Whisk in the remaining sugar. Fold into the cheese mixture.
5. Peel, core and thinly slice the pear and put into the prepared pastry shell. Spoon the cheese mixture over it. Place the tin on a baking tray and bake in the oven at 220°C/425°F/Gas Mark 7 for 20 minutes. Lower the oven temperature to 180°C/350°F/Gas Mark 4 for a further 35-50 minutes, or until the cheesecake is golden brown and set. Cool in the tin.
6. Serve warm dusted with icing sugar and decorated with sugared flowers.

BAKED STRAWBERRY CHEESECAKE

SERVES 6-8

75 g (3 oz) self-raising flour
25 g (1 oz) cornflour
75 g (3 oz) butter, diced
milk for mixing
115 g (4 oz) strawberries, hulled and sliced
225 g (8 oz) medium-fat curd cheese
50 g (2 oz) caster sugar
2 eggs, separated
150 ml (5 fl oz) soured cream
whipped cream and caramel shapes (see Cook's Tip on page 76), to decorate

1. Put the flour and cornflour in a bowl. Rub in the butter until the mixture resembles fine breadcrumbs, then add a little milk to bind.
2. Roll out the pastry on a lightly floured surface and use to line a 23 cm (9 in) spring-release cake tin. Chill for 15 minutes. Bake blind in the oven at 200°C/400°F/Gas Mark 6 for 10 minutes, then remove the paper and beans and bake for a further 10-15 minutes until the base is crisp and golden brown.
3. Arrange the strawberries on top of the pastry shell.
4. Blend together the curd cheese, sugar, egg yolks and soured cream. Whisk the egg whites until stiff, then gently fold into the mixture. Pour on top of the strawberries and bake in the oven at 180°C/350°F/Gas Mark 4 for 40-45 minutes until firm. Serve hot or cool.
5. To serve, remove from tin and decorate with whipped cream and caramel shapes.

Easter Cheesecake